Running For My Life

Captive of the RUF Rebels of Sierra Leone

By

Fr. Victor F.M. Mosele, SX

Published by
E. T. NEDDER PUBLISHING
TUCSON, ARIZONA

Photo credits: *front cover, top photo:* © Daniel Conteh; *bottom photo:*
© 1999, *The Washington Post*. Photo by Michel DuCille. Reprinted
with permission; *back cover* (photo with Pope Paul II):
© *L'Osservatore Romano*. Reprinted with permission.

The Book Team:
Ernie Nedder, Publisher
Kathy Nedder, CFO
Father Victor Mosele, SX, Author
Kate Harrison, Editor
Sharon Nicks, Designer

Additional copies of this publication may be purchased by sending
check or money order for (in U.S.) $18 (paperback) or $25
(hardcover) to: Theological Book Service, P.O. Box 509, Barnhart, MO
63012. Or call toll free 1-888-247-3023. Fax: 1-800-325-9526. E-mail:
bookstore@theobooks.org. Be sure to check our Web site for a list of
other products: www.nedderpublishing.com.

Individual copies in U.S.: $18 (paperback); $25 (hardcover)
Multiple copy discounts available.

ISBN: 978-1-893757-52-3
ISBN: 1-893757-52-8

DEDICATION

*Dedicated with gratitude and love
to the many people in Sierra Leone
who risked their lives to aid me
during my captivity and escape.*

*Their selfless daring made my ordeal less difficult
and ultimately resulted in my deliverance.*

*I can only hope to return to their beautiful country
and reciprocate, at least in part, their kindness.*

CONTENTS

ACKNOWLEDGMENTS

I wish to thank Judy Windover, Kathleen O'Brian, and Ben Moga for their generous assistance in reviewing and correcting the manuscript at different stages of its formation. Gratitude also is expressed to Peter Ivaska, Nick Blaha, and Brian Fink for reading over the text and offering many useful suggestions.

A very special thanks must go to Sr. Mary Kathleen Glavich, SND, for taking the time to do a complete and final revision of the manuscript, in spite of her tight schedule as an established author of more than 40 books. She also found a publisher and led me along the intricate process of publishing a book. Without her encouragement, at a critical time when I was about to give up, this book would have never seen the light of day.

Thanks also to my dear friend and benefactor of our Missions in Sierra Leone, Mr. Peter Heiler, CEO of MAP ART, Oshawa, Toronto, Canada, who put me in touch with Srs. Mary Dion Horrigan, SND, and Kathleen Glavich and offered me encouragement and financial assistance.

Finally I must acknowledge the warm support and encouragement of my Xaverian Missionary Society in the U.S. and particularly my own community at Xavier Knoll, Franklin, Wis. They always materially and spiritually backed me up in my constant travels and ministry in promoting Catholic Foreign

Missions awareness in the people of God, particularly among college students.

If any error or literary barbarism is found in the text, I must take full responsibility for it, since I have entered several additions after the final revision of the script.

FOREWORD

War makes human beings less human. Father Victor
Mosele's story, *Running for My Life – Captive of the RUF Rebels of
Sierra Leone*, is a telling account of the dehumanizing effect of
war on combatants. War divides people into good and bad,
friends and enemies, with the underlying philosophy that the
bad have to be destroyed and the enemies crushed. In spite of
official declarations to the contrary, in times of war life becomes
cheap, violence is the order of the day, and often the ends justify
the means.

Civilians are those who suffer most in time of war. Most
casualties are civilians. In the Sierra Leone war, wanton
destruction and unspeakable atrocities were unleashed by
fighting forces on civilian targets and civilian populations. Yet
the best examples of courage, loyalty, generosity and dignity
came from the civilians.

Father Mosele has been a witness of both the degradation
of the rebels' humanity and the quiet dignity of his civilian
friends. The account of his first and second capture and the
description of the subsequent ordeals is an important document
not only for the historical record of the war in Sierra Leone, but
also for the lessons that may be learned.

The first lesson is that with war there are no winners, only losers. Loss of life and limbs, destruction of private property and public facilities cut across the dividing line of opposite factions. Family life is disrupted, education stopped, economic activity strangled. Fear, insecurity, suspicions, and accusations distort mutual relationships. Moral values break down. Father Mosele testifies that lying, stealing, killing, raping, and other atrocities were a way of life for the fighters.

As a consequence, another lesson to learn is that war should be banned from the world as a means to solve national or international disputes. This includes a ban on small arms and on the illegal flow of weapons. Dialogue, negotiations, political settlements are the way to solve problems. We have to change the old axiom "If you want peace, prepare for war" into: "If you want peace, prepare for peace." From the wisdom of our elders we learn that "you do not put out fire with fire."

We must learn also to discover and to address the underlying causes of war. Most conflicts arise from unbearable situations of injustice, oppression, denial of human rights and freedoms, extreme poverty, corruption, bad governance. Such situations become fertile ground for social unrest, the rise of fundamentalism and the exploitation of religious or ethnic differences. The late Holy Father Pope John Paul II has often said, "If you want peace work for justice, promote human rights, and respect creation." In his last New Year's message he gave us a full treatise on the way to maintain peace in the word. Peace will be achieved by removing the causes of war.

Father Mosele's story ends with a message of hope. The loyalty, support, generosity and love received from many friends, including some rebel fighters, sustained him in his most difficult moments. It is one more demonstration that evil can be overcome by good. And it is the last lesson we learn from this story, which I like to express in the words of John Paul II: "Evil is never defeated by evil . . . Peace is a good to be promoted by good."

"Do not be overcome by evil, but overcome evil with good."
(Rm. 12:21)

+ George Biguzzi, SX
Bishop of Makeni, Sierra Leone, West Africa
Sept. 21, 2005

MAP OF SIERRA LEONE
AFRICA

INTRODUCTION

For decades, hundreds of thousands of men, women, and children have suffered and died without mercy because of the fighting in Africa. From east to west, north to south, Africa is a continent of great political and religious unrest.

Twenty years ago, Sierra Leone, a republic on the Atlantic coast of West Africa, south of Guinea/Conakry and north of Liberia, was drawn into a civil war as part of a wider regional conflict. Corporal Foday Sankoh, instigated and aided by foreign elements (mainly Libya and Liberia) that had entirely different goals and ideologies than his own, started a revolutionary movement against both alleged and real corruption of the legitimate government. This revolution was characterized by widespread atrocities perpetrated on innocent civilians. Among other things, rebels hacked off limbs, gouged out eyes, and quartered living bodies. They also kidnapped thousands of children and induced them to fight as soldiers.

The official name of the rebels of Sierra Leone was the Revolutionary United Front (RUF). Possibly various revolutionary groups in Sierra Leone, for reasons unrelated to foreign influence, began subversion and then united under the leadership of Sankoh. Another possible genesis of the RUF is that a disgruntled Sankoh, swayed by outside influence, recruited other seditious elements in Liberia and Sierra Leone and formed some sort of union, hence the Revolutionary *United* Front. Be that as it may, the fact was obvious that often the RUF rebels were anything but united.

Running for My Life – Captive of the RUF Rebels of Sierra Leone is a true account of my being captured twice by the Revolutionary United Front. I am a Catholic missionary priest originally from Italy. Since 1952, I have been a member of the St. Francis Xavier Foreign Mission Society, whose world headquarters are in Parma, Italy. Our main office in the United States is in Wayne, N.J. I trained in the United States and worked as a priest for 12 years before being assigned to Sierra Leone in 1971. There I witnessed roughly 30 years of political, cultural and religious growth and upheaval.

While in Africa I held many roles, such as school builder, teacher, nurse, parish priest and prison chaplain in several towns and villages of different tribes. My last assignment was that of parish priest of the Mission post of Kambia. I managed 33 grade schools for about 6,000 children in the Kambia District, a position that lasted five years. Then I was captured twice, with an interlude of 10 months, and held prisoner for a total of five months before escaping. I still pray and hope to return to my Mission in Sierra Leone. This is my story.

PLEASE NOTE: *For security purposes, all names of the living in this account have been changed, except the names of public figures and missionaries.*

+Victor F. Mosele, SX

CHAPTER ONE

The Blitz of Kambia and the First Capture

Thursday night, Feb. 11, 1999:

The Noisy Attack on Kambia

10:45 p.m. The front door was closed and barricaded, as it has been every night for the last three years. The steel door at the back of the house was also locked. Father Franco Manganello, who was forced to abandon his mission at Madina and was now staying with me, had long since retired. Even the two Mission boys, Sheku and one nicknamed Bimbo, had lain down. I got into my pajamas and, relaxing in my reclining chair, fell into a peaceful slumber. Suddenly in my light sleep I heard the ta-ta-ta-ta- of automatic rifles coming from far away.

I bolted up, turned on the battery-operated bedside lamp, and looked at my watch—11:30 p.m. Ta-ta-ta-ta, poon-ta-poonpoon-poon, ta-ta-ta-ta-ta. The sounds of rifles, machine guns, and rocket-propelled grenades were coming from the direction of the checkpoint, approximately one mile straight southeast of the Mission. The checkpoint was a new suburban development of Kambia that took its name from a military or police barrier/post, which had been in place there off and on through the years. At that time, Guinean soldiers of the

ECOMOG (West Africa Community peacekeeping force) had their checkpoint in place there, controlling the flux of people coming from the Port Loko District into the Kambia District. They also controlled the long Chinese-built bridge spanning the Kolenten River (the Great Scarcies), which led to the Guinean/ Sierra Leone border five miles away.

The sound of the automatic weapons was continuous, interrupted only by the explosions of mortars and multiple grenade launchers. I quickly dressed in my running clothes, neatly folded at the foot of the bed, always ready, as they had been for the past three years on account of past rebel incursions and the constant threat of more of the same. Also set to go was my backpack containing essentials such as personal documents, medical supplies, a knife and minimal clothing. I tossed my portable radio into the backpack and rushed to Father Franco's room, knocking loudly. He answered, "I'm coming!" The boys were already on their feet and ready to go. Downstairs in my office I grabbed the satellite phone that the organization Caritas had brought to the mission to recharge its battery. I pushed the phone into my backpack and rushed to the radio room. I wrapped our transmitter in a foam rubber sheet, put it in a nylon bag, and handed it to Bimbo. Fifteen minutes after the first report of gunfire, still going on, we left the house.

Outside the back door Pa Abu Kamara, our watchman, was waiting in consternation. I reassured him, "There is nothing to panic about. The shooting is still far away. We have plenty of time to walk to the riverside and hide in the thick bush." On the way out of the Mission compound we stopped by the abandoned chassis of a pickup truck that had been pushed into a corner. We buried the radio transmitter under the dry leaves trapped in the chassis before heading to the north gate of the compound. I said to the watchman, "Pa, come on, open the gate!" He mumbled, "The keys! I left the keys on the church veranda." The church was only 100 feet away. "Go and get them," I said. He didn't move. He was immobilized by fear. I was about to go myself when I noticed that Father Franco was already walking toward the far end of the compound.

In order to exit the Mission area in that direction, one must climb a small wall. Well then, I decided, we could go that way. The obstacle was minimal; anyone could jump the wall with no problem. Unfortunately, as Father Franco jumped down, one of the boys jumped a split second after him, crashing on him in a three-foot-deep ditch, which perhaps both of them in the darkness hadn't seen. The priest was injured; however, no one noticed it at first. He got up quickly without uttering a sound since his adrenaline was pumping.

We were on the road past the Mission compound, Kumraby Dura Road. After a few feet we turned left off the road into the brush and crept past houses and backyards, heading to the riverside about 300 yards away. We realized that we were walking with many other people, all following the same escape route in total silence. Around us all was quiet except for the faraway, unabated roar of gunfire.

By midnight we were in the middle of high grass and thick brush by the river. Because we were in the dry season and the rapids were shallow, we could easily wade across the river to continue our escape. But not yet: the shooting was still far away, and didn't seem to get any closer. Nothing fell anywhere around us—no bullets and no shells. We guessed that the Guinean soldiers were the ones shooting, holding up the rebels coming from the direction of Port Loko. We lay in the bush waiting, listening and watching in wonder at the tracer bullets in the sky and the flashes of explosions. I looked back, straining my eyes into the dark, to find Father Franco. I made out his shape. He was standing, leaning against a big tree. I crawled to him, tapped him on his shoulder, and whispered, "Come, lie down in the nice spot I've found." He didn't respond. I surmised that he must be terrified and returned to my hole and lay down.

As the shooting and the flashes of light continued faraway, someone in the crowd suggested going to the nearby houses, less than 75 yards away down the riverside, to find more comfortable quarters. We all agreed and crossed the wild brush in silence and darkness to the houses. I turned to look for Father Franco, but he was nowhere to be seen. I called softly, but there was no answer. I asked Sheku, then Bimbo if they had seen him. Nobody had. Then I told the boys, "Go back and look for Father."

Shortly they returned to tell me that Father was halfway back, crouched down in the brush, by a tree, unable to walk. Some strong men in the group volunteered to go back with the boys, while I held onto Father's bags and mine.

Less than five minutes later they returned, half carrying, half dragging Father Franco. He was in great distress and unable to stand by himself. He moaned and muttered repeatedly, "My leg, oh, oh, oh, my leg." We tried to lay him down on the closest veranda, but that caused him more agony. He cried and begged, "Let me be. Leave me alone. Let me see if I can find a way. Slow, slow, ah, ah!" After he reached a seemingly more bearable position, he breathed heavily and muttered, "If only I had something, an injection, a Baralgine injection." Later we learned that he had suffered a hip fracture.

I don't carry Baralgine (a potent painkiller) in my medical kit, but only malaria remedies, a snakebite kit, some bandages, aspirin, and Panadol (Paracetamol). On the suggestion of Sheku, we helped Father inside the house and laid him on a mat in the pavement. I gave him two 500 mg tablets of Panadol with some water. While I held his head, he swallowed and nearly choked on the tablets. He was in a cold sweat. When he breathed heavily again, we laid his head on a pillow provided by someone of the house, but Father amidst his moanings muttered in Italian, "This pillow stinks terribly of excrements. Please remove it." Having nothing else to prop his head with, I removed a clean towel from my bag, wrapped the pillow, and placed it under his head again.

Outside, far away, all hell was breaking loose; and inside Father was restless. Men and women crowded into the little room, expressing sympathy and solidarity. There was nothing else they could do. The shooting was unabated but still not closing in. So I decided to attempt returning to the Mission to get a vial of Baralgine and a syringe. Father Franco whispered between moans, "No, don't go back, don't go back." But my mind was made up. I had to go.

Friday morning, Feb. 12:
The Quiet Invasion of Kambia—My Capture

It was 6:30 a.m.—still dark and the shooting still going on. I couldn't tell who was shooting, but I felt reasonably sure that there were no rebels in town, much less near the Mission. That's why I decided to return to it for Baralgine. I called Bimbo, and he, Pa Abu, and I retraced our steps toward the Mission. Except for the distant explosions, all was quiet in our immediate surroundings. Not a living soul was in sight. We reached the Mission's north gate, which was locked as we left it.

I said to Bimbo, "Here is the flashlight. Go to the east gate and jump over the low wall next to it. Go up to the veranda of the church, get the keys, and come open the gate for us."

Just as he took off and I was looking absentmindedly toward the western corner of the Mission compound, a dark mass of moving people suddenly and silently materialized out of the semidarkness from Kumraby Dura Road. It was the rebels— about 40 of them, approaching quietly, dressed in rags with heavy guns in their hands and cartridge bandoliers across their chests. It was too late to run. Seeing no way to escape, I faced up to them. Taking a few steps forward I called, "Good morning, gentlemen. Can I help you?"

On seeing me come forward so unexpectedly, they were momentarily taken aback. Then some of them rushed forward. One declared: "You are under arrest!" and began to frisk me.

"Wait a minute," I said. "What are you doing? I am the Father in the Mission here. I'm a priest."

From somewhere in the group a voice thundered, "Let him be. Don't you see? He is the priest!"

Presently the man who issued the order came forward, dressed in rags like the rest. Later I learned that he was Colonel Kumba Bundama, commander of the RUF.

He asked, "Are you the priest here?"

"Yes."

"Do you have a satellite phone?"

"No, I don't."

"Do you have any money, dollars?"

"No, not in this mission."

"The gate. Open up!" he commanded.

"I don't have the key," I said. "I've just sent a boy to get it."

At that instant a shot thundered from right behind me, and a rebel shouted, "Eh! There's an armed man out there at the church." Two more shattering bangs in rapid succession deafened me.

"It is not an armed man," I said loudly. "It is the boy I sent to retrieve the key to the gate. He's holding a flashlight not a gun."

A couple of rebels jumped the chain-link fence and ran after the supposedly armed man. I learned later that Bimbo outwitted the rebels, escaped, and went in a roundabout path to the riverside. There he reported my capture to Father Franco and the rest of the group.

Meanwhile, a rebel shot open the padlock. The rebels invaded the Mission compound, and the commander instructed me to open all the doors. After retrieving the keys from the church veranda, I opened the garage doors, the back entry to the house itself, the kitchen, the pantry, the various offices, and the upstairs bedrooms. The rebels took everything they could grab and carry. The commander shouted to one carrying the television set, its electrical cables dragging, "Make sure you take note of every item removed from here because everything will have to be returned!" What a farce! I knew nothing would be returned.

Everything was brought down into the backyard where the Mission's vehicles were parked. In the office the books were dumped off the shelves, scattered on the floor, and kicked around. The rebels were looking for money in or behind the books, in the drawers, the cupboards, and the closets. They found nothing, but the damage and chaos they created were beyond description.

In the courtyard they loaded their loot haphazardly onto the three Mission vehicles. Everything happened quickly and almost in silence. At one point a boy, a child-soldier—no more than 12 or 13 years old and toting a heavy AK-47 rifle taller than he—approached, holding a small bundle neatly wrapped in newspaper. I recognized the packet of four lumps of butter I had bought in Conakry, Guinea, a week earlier and had placed in the freezer. (For two years Conakry, the capital of Guinea, had become our only source of provisions. We could no longer travel to Freetown, the capital of Sierra Leone, because all the area between it and Kambia was a war zone and impassable.)

"It's butter," I said. He bit on the bundle without even removing the paper and exclaimed, "It's so hard and cold!" "My boy, it's frozen," I gently explained. He looked at me quizzically and boasted, "But I am a rebel. I am strong!" With that, he strutted away.

The loading was complete. Nothing else would fit. The commander spoke. "Let's go. You, too, Father, must come with us."

"Me?" I questioned. "Why do you want me? What do you expect from me?"

He spoke without looking at me. "Do not worry. No harm will come to you. We will release you very soon."

Pa Abu was standing next to me, frozen with fear. I asked the colonel, "What about this man? He is too old to be of any use to you. Let him go."

Looking at the man and then at me, the colonel asked, "Who is he?"

"He's our watchman," I answered.

"Okay," he barked to Pa Abu. "Go!"

Pa took off like an arrow. I had never seen him move so fast. The convoy of the three vehicles moved out of the Mission, heading toward Kukuna Road. Shooting continued at the checkpoint. In town there was not a living soul.

We crossed town, heading toward Madina, passing Kolenten Secondary School and the Polio Rehabilitation Center. In less than five minutes we reached the small village of 'Kpairoh. In the center of the village, the colonel stopped and ordered the trucks off the road. On a level piece of ground everything was unloaded. I sat on a stone by the side and watched the operation, contemplating all the things looted and now piled up like junk. As soon as the pickups were emptied, the colonel ordered a return trip to Kambia for more pillaging. At one point Lieutenant Jacob tossed me a small radio, saying, "Have this. It will help you to divert your mind from what you are seeing." All day, from 8 a.m. to 9 p.m., the vehicles came and went, unloading large amounts of things that eventually, in the following days, would be carried to the rebel base in Kamakwie. In the sky over Kambia I could see tall columns of smoke rising up. They were burning the town.

During that day, more trucks were found and commandeered, as well as a dozen or so motorcycles. Most were looted from Action Aid, a British NGO (Non-Government Organization). On all of them the ignition switches were bashed in and the wires crossed. The drivers came racing at 60 or 70 mph into the village from Kambia, shouting as if drunk or drugged. Among other things, the trucks brought in twelve 50-gallon drums of fuel. The shooting at the checkpoint continued.

I learned later that the attack on Kambia was carried out by two groups of rebels, part of a contingent made up of rebels from Lunsar and Kamakwie, south and southeast of Kambia, respectively. The rebels had split into two groups perhaps at the Mecca junction, about two miles southeast of Kambia, on the Port Loko road. One group, possibly the largest, went directly toward the checkpoint, where they were stopped and held back by the Guinean soldiers based there. This is where the heavy fire was coming from. The smaller group quietly bypassed the checkpoint, cut behind the old English Reservation, where all the district officers had their quarters, and stole into town by way of Kumraby Dura Road.

Around midday trays of cooked rice were brought from Kambia. The warriors took turns eating. On being invited, I sat around one of the trays with seven or eight rebels and ate, scooping the rice up by hand. The rebels opened a bag of cans of beer, obviously looted from some bar. They all ate and drank merrily. I too helped myself to a couple of beers, but not merrily. I had to drink something—there was no water around!

By nightfall the sky over Kambia was blanketed in smoke.

I wondered about the Mission and the church and asked the colonel about it. He assured me that the fires were not houses burning, but grass fires in the fields around town. Actually, we were in the dry season when people did set grass on fire to clean and clear the land for the planting season, but I knew that the colonel was lying. I was overwhelmed with sadness thinking of the wanton destruction of houses, facilities and property.

Friday night. Feb. 12:
First Leg of the Journey to Makeni

At about 10 p.m. the colonel gave orders that Captain Blood (the battle name of the young rebel Abu Kanneh), Lieutenant Jacob, and four other rebels accompany me to Madina with the Mission's Land Rover, while other fighters would follow in a pickup, also the Mission's. Both vehicles were loaded to the bursting point with all sorts of things thrown in and shoved together: televisions, videos, car batteries, fuel cans, tools, small motors, toys and furniture.

We took off at 11:30 p.m. After 10 miles the pickup broke down with tire problems. No wonder, with that overload! Nothing could be done, so the Land Rover continued alone. We reached Madina about 1 a.m. We passed the Catholic Mission compound, which had been vandalized by the rebels three weeks earlier. In the center of town, at the intersection of the road for Kamakwie, we stopped. The streets were abandoned.

Captain Blood left the vehicle, walked to a nearby building, and knocked heavily on a big door. This must be a store, I thought. He knocked and shouted until the door opened. Those inside must have been collaborators, either willing or forced. There were apologies and greetings while arrangements were made to unload everything and for all of us to spend the rest of the night in that house. A young man from the house offered me his room. We entered by candlelight and I dropped, fully dressed, on the bed. Two sleepless nights plus all the excitement overwhelmed me. I was done in and fell asleep in no time.

I woke up to light filtering through the window panels. People (rebels, I guessed) began to come into the room without hesitation. One opened the window, and I realized that I had to get up. Rubbing my eyes and scratching myself because of the bedbugs, I staggered outdoors. In front of the house a large number of people were assembled, talking and whispering. When they saw me, they all fell silent and stared. I advanced and greeted a few. They took courage. Some were Catholics. They returned my greeting and expressed sympathy. When they offered food, I declined but asked for coffee. There was none. They brought me tea instead.

When Lieutenant Jacob came out of the house, I asked him if I could visit the nearby Catholic Mission. He agreed and detailed two of his orderlies to follow me with their guns. With David Yillah, an ex-seminarian functioning as catechist in Madina, and Peter, the headmaster of our school there, we walked to the Mission, about 200 yards away. As we entered the Mission's building, it looked like the aftermath of a hurricane.

There was no need to open any door since all were bashed in and everything was scattered on the floor: clothes, books, implements, pots and pans, tools and broken glass. To go anywhere I had to walk over everything. I couldn't even push it aside, so thick a mess had piled up.

I walked into the small kitchen and noticed with surprise that the small gas stove was still in place. I checked the gas tank and found it full. Searching the floor I found a small pack of coffee and a coffee pot half buried under the debris, and congratulated myself on the opportunity to make a good cup of coffee. It would be the last one for months.

Coffee cup in hand, I went to Father Franco's bedroom. It was havoc. The mattress was gone, clothes were strewn all over the floor, and half-unfurled rolls of toilet paper streaked the floor in all directions. There was an eerie air of a nightmare.

I walked on to the pharmacy of Brothers Bruno and Guri's mobile clinic. This occupied the central section of the Mission house. The brothers were stationed at Madina, forming a community with Father Franco. Even before I entered the pharmacy area, I was stepping over capsules, pills, syringes, gauze and the like. The steel door of the pharmacy was still in place and locked, but it was battered and chewed up around the handle. I don't know how many heavy caliber bullets were wasted on it, but the door hadn't budged. Eventually they must have used the sledgehammer that was still lying on the floor to knock down one section of the cement block wall, thus creating a passage. I entered the pharmacy store through that hole.

The shelves were empty. The floor was completely covered with empty boxes of the various medicines; nothing to salvage, a total loss. The end of the world! I got out of there. The church was adjacent to the house. I entered it through the back door, which was still in place. Not bad. The church had not been tampered with; there were just some bullet marks here and there, obviously shot from the outside.

When we returned to the house where I'd slept, I met with David and the headmaster. They told me all about the night of the attack. Most of it I knew already from Father Franco's account. While they were talking and the rebels were busy with their arrangements, I inspected the surroundings attentively but hoping to appear nonchalant, thinking of a possible escape. The rebels must have suspected as much. I noticed several armed men and child-soldiers posted at four corners about 200 yards from the shop/house.

I knew that the big town of Kukuna was only eight miles away to the east and that one mile beyond Kukuna was the Guinean border. Earlier in the day I had mentioned to David the possibility of an escape. He was ready to lead me. However, now he told me that he'd sought advice from trusted members of the church, and they cautioned that if I escaped, the rebels might retaliate by burning down the town. I had to admit that it was certainly plausible. At that prospect, I decided that my escape was not worth the cost of so much property and possible loss of human life.

While I stood at the entrance of the house, patiently waiting for time to pass, a couple of trucks filled with rebels en route from Kamakwie to Kambia stopped for a break. Although I knew many of the rebels personally, these I did not. One of them, dressed in rags with bandoliers hanging across his chest and a heavy bayoneted gun in his hand, saw me and shouted, "Who are you? Get inside there and lay low. It's time we teach you white men your place!"

I tried to say something, but the boy leveled his gun at me. I figured it was better to go inside. After the incident his buddies must have told him that I was a missionary priest, because, as I was sitting on the bed, somewhat mortified, the same warrior came in and said, "Hello, Father." He added apologetically, while embracing me and patting me on the back, "Don't worry, Father. Don't be afraid!" I returned the kindness by whispering, "I understand."

The rebels served me food, good food—rice and chicken prepared by a kind, middle-aged woman, a member of our church. Evening came. When it was dark, I lay down and tried to sleep.

CHAPTER TWO

On the Way to Kamakwie

Just as I was about to fall asleep, Captain Blood came in and said, "We must leave for Kamakwie right now. Orders from the colonel." I got up and, having nothing to prepare or pack, walked out into the dark. The Land Rover was ready, overloaded as before. The captain said, "You drive, Father. Lieutenant Jacob, give the keys to Father!"

I got into the driver's seat, and two other men squeezed in next to me. Four others sat in the backseat; and others hung on the outside, on the side and back doors. As I shifted into first gear, I heard and felt the engine moan with its load. We drove into the night toward Kamakwie, quickly leaving Madina behind. The road, if it could be called that, was atrocious. I decided to engage the auxiliary four-wheel drive.

An hour later we met a stalled Honda XI 125 motorcycle attended by a rebel. It was broken down. After a few words of explanation from the rider, the captain ordered, "Load it up!" Flabbergasted, I cried, "But where?"

The captain calmly said to me, "On the roof." Then, to the rider, "And you, Alpha, get on with it, to hold it in place." If The Land Rover didn't break down then, it never would! I bitterly recalled the nearly $500 I'd spent only one month before to install four new Michelin tires! The Land Rover held on and trudged along.

We crossed over the Great Scarcies River on a ferry, hand-hauled. After that, we ran into a flock of sheep and goats. Captain Blood shouted, "Stop! Stop! Let's grab a goat to take along!" I hadn't a clue where he would put the goat. Before we even came to a halt, a couple of the young rebels who had been hanging onto the side doors were already running after the frightened goats. But the men must have been too tired, as they couldn't catch a single animal. With a curse, the captain ordered, "Blow the horn. Let's move!" The chase stopped and the two rebels scrambled up the side of the vehicle. Thanks be to God! I supposed he would have placed the captured goat on my lap!

By three in the morning we arrived at Kamakwie. At rebels' headquarters loud music and carousing were in full swing. Young men and women milled around in a large courtyard. Almost everyone was smoking and drinking, and the scent of marijuana hung in the air. Captain Blood led me into a rambling house through a maze of darkened corridors into a rather spacious and well lit room full of young ladies, music and smoke. One king-sized bed and four large easy chairs occupied most of it. Nobody seemed to pay any attention to me, but the captain was greeted with excitement, hugs and kisses. In the middle of all the commotion he communicated through motions and a voice drowned in the noise to sit down and make myself comfortable. However, there was no empty place. I was about to squeeze onto the armrest of the nearest chair, when the girl sitting on it got up, leaving it all for me.

I was so tired that the hustle and bustle around me didn't bother me much. I simply let it happen, waiting to be given a place to lie down. But nobody seemed to care. At one point the captain told me to relax and pointed to the bed where three of the girls were frolicking. I stood up and shouted in his ear, trying to overcome the music, "Captain, don't you think this is the wrong place for me to lie down?" "Oh yeah," he said, "You're right. Come with me." He took me out of there and into an adjacent building in a darkened and relatively quiet room with another large bed occupied by a young man. Too tired to engage in small talk, I curtly greeted the man, who was half-asleep anyway, I thanked the captain and dropped onto the bed. I was gone.

I woke up with the light in my eyes. I guessed it must have been around 8 a.m. Peeping through the window, I saw small movements: boys and girls were roaming through the courtyard, half-dressed and still half asleep. By following the direction of their movements, I located an outhouse. After making use of it, still in a daze, I looked around for the Land Rover. I spotted it among other cars and trucks and went to it, trying to make a connection in that strange place. There was no sign of the rebels who captured me; in fact, those moving around didn't look like fighters, although some were carelessly toting guns.

Sunday morning, Feb. 14:
Last Stretch to Makeni

By 9 a.m. Captain Blood showed up accompanied by several noisy rebels. Almost immediately a *palaver* (heated argument) broke out—one of the many that I would witness among the rebels throughout my captivity. This one was over the fuel they looted in Kambia. Other trucks had arrived from Kambia during the night. The fuel was stocked in several 50-gallon drums and five-gallon plastic containers.

"Give me 10 gallons!"

"Give me five gallons!"

"No, this is mine!"

"I am in charge here."

Soon the shouting turned into pushing, pulling, cursing and gun pointing. Finally, a major intervened, pistol in hand. Then, two quick shots into the air and an imperious, "Shut up, all you rabble! Nobody touches nothing. All this has to go to Makeni. This is final! Load up and let's go!" By 10 a.m. we were ready to move. That included the Land Rover plus a large six-ton truck. We left Kamakwie behind us, traveling a road that was all holes and rutted tracks left over from the previous rain season. On the way we came to Kamalu, one of our oldest Mission posts. This was Father Mario Guerra's Mission. He had been beaten up and abducted some two months earlier, following its looting and destruction.

I begged Captain Blood to stop and let me visit the ravaged

house and church. He consented. Earlier on, even as we were approaching the town, I saw many people staring at the Land Rover as it passed by. Seeing me, a white man with a beard at the wheel, they thought I was Father Mario and waved excitedly. Now that we were nearing the Mission on foot, I heard voices from afar saying, "Father Mario is back." I waved and went toward the church. Just then a large group of parishioners were coming out after a Sunday service. They immediately greeted me, saying, "Father Mario!" But then they were startled, and someone said, "No, it's Father Victor!" They had heard from the BBC radio about my capture. The catechist came forward, calling my name and offering his hand. "Sorry, Father Victor, how are you?"

"I'm OK," I reassured them. "Don't worry about me. Everything will be all right. How are you doing?"

The people were all smiles now. The catechist said, "Father, we are managing. As you can see, the Mission has been reduced to rubble, but we continue to pray and gather for the Word of God. All our hopes are in Him, Father."

They asked me if I needed anything and whether I had been mistreated. I reassured them again that I was fine. Things will soon become normal, I said. They all listened, but clearly their apprehension was not allayed. The thought occurred to me that this was a good opportunity to escape, since Kamalu is not too far from the forest or from the Guinean border, and these people would certainly help. But then again, what about the consequences to the town after my escape, assuming that it were successful? I put away the thought of escape, rejecting it as a temptation. I'll escape, I told myself, only if and when others will not be victimized for my actions.

After inspecting the Mission's compound, the Fathers' residence and the church, all of which were in shambles, I walked back to the Land Rover accompanied by a fairly large group of Christians, perhaps 40 or 50. After parting from them, we headed toward Makeni. At Pendembu we stopped for lunch. The captain bought all of us some roast wild beef from a street vendor. We sat on the veranda of a house in front of the big mosque. Captain Blood offered me some table wine from a carton, the last of the wine looted from our Mission in Kambia. I accepted it gratefully, because I couldn't bring myself to drink the local water, which looked as if it hadn't been purified by either boiling or chlorine tablets.

Ever since we'd left Kamakwie, one of the rebels had sat on the roof of the big truck filled with fuel drums that traveled ahead of the Land Rover. He searched the sky for any Nigerian Air Force Alpha Jet of the ECOMOG peacekeeping forces that would intermittently patrol the area and bomb or machine-gun any moving vehicle, whether on or off the road. So far, all had been clear.

CHAPTER THREE

At Makeni, Before the RUF High Command

By 4 p.m. we reached Makeni, the capital of the Bombali District and of the Northern Province of Sierra Leone. At the first rebel checkpoint before entering the city, at a location called Pamlap, my captors entered the post house, a command center for their forces, and were served food. They called me in and invited me to eat with them. Although I was in no mood for food, I ate as much as necessary, both not to irritate my captors and to survive.

As we were about to move on to enter Makeni, I willingly gave up the driver's seat of my Land Rover to the major, who had been riding in the fuel truck. He obviously wanted to show off driving into town, although it was clear that he was not an experienced driver. I was well known by most people in Makeni. Now, a captive, I didn't relish being seen entering the city at the wheel of my own vehicle filled with smiling rebels, as if I were a willing member of the gang. So, I purposely sat in the middle, keeping a straight face, and did not look out the windows.

We went through familiar streets and passed familiar places. We crossed the town through Independence Square and into Rogbane Road and Lunsar Road. When we reached the first side street leading to the official residence of the Xaverian Missionaries in Sierra Leone, called "The Religious House," we turned left. On that street and about 150 yards ahead, we arrived at a large house recently built by some rich Sierra Leonean who was probably engaged in the diamond business. Now, vacated of its rightful owner, the house had become the residence of Brigadier General Jussu Kamara, RUF, the commander of several thousand rebels in the Northern Province. He was a young man of 25 who, I was later told, attended one year at our own St. Francis Secondary School, where I was then teaching, right across the street from his present residence.

Captain Blood and his warriors took me to the courtyard, where I found the brigadier general seated on the hood of a Mercedes Benz automobile, surrounded by a large retinue of his own attendants, mostly rebels. I did, however, recognize some Sierra Leone Army soldiers—renegades or deserters—who were still wearing their army uniform and insignia. The area surrounding the house was cluttered with all sorts of stolen or commandeered cars and trucks. I stepped forward to greet the general and to introduce myself. I extended my hand and, as pleasantly as I could muster, said, "Hello, good afternoon, Brigadier General, sir. I am Father Victor Mosele, abducted from the Catholic Mission in Kambia and brought here against my will." I made it a point to state this openly and clearly, lest my presence there be misunderstood. Remaining seated, Brigadier

Jussu greeted me without warmth, not shaking hands and scarcely looking at me.

I tried to warm him up by congratulating and thanking him for his good deeds in protecting the priests and sisters in Makeni during the first rebel occupation of that city the previous year. I couldn't tell if he appreciated my remarks. I learned later that I had confused him with one Brigadier General James, who took an active part in defending and somewhat protecting the 40-odd priests, brothers, sisters, catechists, and others who were confined at the Pastoral Center of Makeni during of the first occupation of the city. This had been a 17-day nightmare when the town was plundered and partially burned down and saw heavy loss of lives.

Brigadier Jussu, still sitting on the hood, said coldly, "You have not been abducted. My men rescued you from the dangers of the ECOMOG forces. We were concerned for your safety." I rejoined that in Kambia I was not in any danger from the ECOMOG forces; they never touched nor harassed me. It was his men who came in to burn and cause havoc. I tried to be facetious. "I have a suggestion to make, Brigadier, sir." I said. "If you can take care of your safety, I believe I can take care of my own." I was smiling but sensed that he did not catch my humor, for in a rather icy voice he said, "Is that so? Very well, go rest for a while. We shall talk more about it later. Perhaps after resting you will make better sense." He detailed two armed men to accompany me to his house and wait for orders.

When I entered the living room of the brigadier's house, the armed men remained outside. Seeing nobody in the room, I sat on the first chair I saw. Looking around, I noticed beautiful appointments, rich carpets, nicely upholstered armchairs, a television as well as video and stereo sets. Through the open back door I saw women and children moving about in the back yard, crouching over pots and pans, cooking on the ground in the typical African fashion.

Suddenly a nicely dressed young lady entered through an inner door and greeted me. I rose and returned the greeting. When she asked me who I was, I told her that I was a Catholic priest, a missionary, captured by the rebels and that I was asked by the brigadier to sit and wait in the house. I learned later that she was his wife. She talked to me very kindly and asked me if I needed anything. I thanked her and added: "I would appreciate having a soft drink and the chance to wash." She asked me to be seated, and, saying that she would see to my requests, departed. Shortly after she had left the room, a middle-aged man in neat attire came in carrying a towel, a pair of slippers, and an orange soda. He indicated a side door where I could go to wash. Thanking him profusely, I took the soft drink and gulped it down. I was so thirsty after five hours of tropical heat and all the excitement. My last drink had been the wine at Pendembu.

When I came out after showering, I found myself in front of a sturdy man in his thirties. He introduced himself in a cheerful manner. "Hello, Father, I am your new bishop!" I was startled.

With a smile he continued, "Brigadier Jussu has asked me to host you in my house that was the bishop's house. I am Colonel Tony Dumbuia. Come with me, please." I followed him outside to a Mercedes Benz. He invited me in the car, and as I was about to board I recognized, some 50 feet away, three important men from the era of previous Sierra Leonean governments: Jonathan Lewis, Anthony Macaully, and another whose name I can't remember. They too were prisoners. The three were involved in an animated discussion and did not take notice of me.

Sunday night, Feb. 14:
My Prison: The Bishop's House

We reached the bishop's house by 7 p.m. As we approached the well-known compound, I could hear loud music, the kind one would expect at a nightclub. I saw men and boys sprawled here and there on the lawn, guns by their side. The building was still intact, with only the doors bashed in. Strange furniture, not the bishop's, cluttered the rooms. Walls, stairway, and floors were smudged by filth; books and papers were strewn all over. The main room upstairs that opened onto the veranda was now set up as a living room. Once it had been spacious and soberly decorated. Now huge sofas and an oblong center table occupied the whole floor, leaving little walking space. Oh, yes, there also were two large refrigerators. Not a single square foot of floor was left open—a good example of "horror vacui" (fear of empty space) reminiscent of rococo art that is crammed with decorations.

There we sat and talked pleasantries for a while. A young man joined us in conversation. He introduced himself as Abdul Richardson Kamara, a Christian Methodist, and former student leader of the opposition at Fourah Bay College, the University of Sierra Leone. He was now a member of the RUF, not a soldier, he said, but a civilian advisor. I learned later that he was the secretary of the RUF intelligence branch, working directly under Lieutenant Colonel John Jarbo, the Head of Intelligence.

Presently, Colonel Tony excused himself, leaving me alone with Abdul. Over the thundering music he explained how, as a student, he had suffered a lot for not receiving adequate help from his immediate family because of poverty. His aunt, who was deputy minister of finance before the revolution started, refused to extend any help to him, but instead lavishly favored her own children, using money from government scholarships and other projects. According to him, government officials were totally corrupt in dispensing aid because of nepotism or for further monetary gains. He narrated to me how he became a leader of the opposition among university students. While at Fourah Bay College, he converted to Christianity from his Muslim faith through the influence of a Methodist pastor who was a Korean missionary. During the coup d'état of the Sierra Leone Army led by Johnny Paul Koroma, Abdul had organized a student movement in support of the new revolution. But when the ousted legitimate government, with the help of the ECOMOG forces, staged a counter-coup, driving J. P. Koroma and the rebels from power and out of Freetown, he ran for his life and formally joined the RUF. He recounted how he became the "theoretician" or philosopher of the revolution, refusing, however, to take up arms because of his Christian principles.

I asked him, "If you refuse to take up arms because of your Christian principles, how do you justify and explain the destruction, the indiscriminate killing, the hacking off of limbs, and the other atrocities that your movement carries out on innocent civilians?"

He answered my question by going into a long dissertation on the roots and dynamics of the RUF revolution (the *movement*, as he called it) and its activities. He attempted to show that whatever the rebels were doing was fully justified; and, in fact, it was an implementation of God's orders, much in the fashion of what happened to the Israelites during the time of the prophet Ezekiel. Of his reasoning and that of the rebels more will be said later in this account. He continued talking above that infernal music coming from a powerful P.A. system looted from some nightclub in town. I began to feel tired. It was dark and must have been about 10 p.m. Suddenly my interlocutor disappeared, offering an excuse I could not understand.

I was left alone and began feeling dazed. As I looked around to size up the situation, two children came in, a boy and girl of six or seven. The girl carried a bowl of rice and a spoon. I thanked them with a smile, and it occurred to me that part of my daze might be due to hunger. I ate ravenously, even though the rice was cold. I left some of it for the children, who gratefully took the bowl and scurried away. Now that my stomach was full, my eyes felt heavy. I wished someone would come to show me where to lie down. They must have forgotten about me, so I stretched out on the sofa and, in spite of the loud music, fell asleep.

CHAPTER FOUR
Life in Detention

The First Day

Early the next morning, three or four loud explosions not too far away woke me up. Then all was silence. It was still dark. Shortly after, I heard quiet movements and soft sounds of people outside the house. This allayed my apprehensions but tickled my curiosity. I reached for my flashlight to check the time. It was 6 a.m. I got up and looked out the window, and in the darkness, I saw only a bright, glowing flame and silhouettes of what I believed were women moving about quickly.

Water? There was none; nothing to wash with, no comb for my hair. Half asleep, I remembered my situation. What was I going to do? Well, I'd wait for daylight. I sat in the easy chair next to the bed, scratching my back, my legs, my head—bedbugs again! Then I switched on the small radio thrown to me by Lieutenant Jacob at Kapairo.

At 6:30 a.m. every day there was a BBC program called "Network Africa." I listened carefully for an announcement of the attack on Kambia, but there was nothing about it. It took 15 days before the BBC announced the incident of Kambia and my capture. That broadcast was from Sylvester Rogers, a BBC correspondent whom I had last seen in Pamelap at the Guinean border three weeks earlier. Six months previous to that last encounter I had helped him escape capture by the junta of J.P. Koroma's army of deserters, the MPRC (Military Provisional Ruling Council). They were seeking him on the charge of passing on reports unfavorable to his government.

Finally, it was daybreak. I combed my hair with my fingers and wiped my face with a small towel I found in the room. I felt the stubble of my beard. This was the fifth day since my last shave. Having heard women's voices in the corridor outside my door and the first notes of pounding, loud music coming from the next room, I ventured out. I saw the colonel and greeted him. Then I said, "Colonel, I must get something to tidy up. Your people have taken everything from me. Could I have some money to go to the market and buy a bar of soap, one or two shirts, a comb, and a shaving kit?" He gave me 9 thousand Leones (= $6.00 in U.S. currency), and detailed two of his guerrillas (with guns at the ready) in addition to theoretician Abdul to escort me to the market.

The bishop's house was about one mile from the market. The first part of the road was empty, but closer to town more and more houses edged it until we were in the thick of town. As we approached the market, we began to hear its clamor of voices and sounds. Making a right turn into Independence Square, we were immediately surrounded by the chaos and noise of the African marketplace. Amid the clutter around small tables, benches, stalls and shops, men, women, and children shouted and chatted, accompanied by the crashes, bangs, and squawking animals associated with selling goods.

As I headed to the thick of this mayhem, followed by the two rebels with leveled guns, the whole market fell into an eerie silence as people gazed at me and at the guns behind me. Previously I had worked for nine years in Makeni as a youth chaplain and as a teacher in the 1,000-strong St. Francis Secondary School. The people must have recognized me even though I was disheveled and dirty – a prisoner of the RUF. I took a few more steps and, with a smile, raised my arm in a cheerful greeting to the onlookers.

It was like pulling a trigger. The whole market crowd burst into clapping and called, "Father Victor! Father Victor!" I felt encouraged and gratified. A surge of emotion filled my throat. Many people came around me smiling, clasping my hands and patting me on the back, greeting me. At first this made my "bodyguards" very nervous, but eventually they calmed down and smiled themselves.

When I moved to start shopping, people, many whom I recognized and others I didn't, offered to help me buy anything I needed. The money the rebels had given me was only about enough for a toothbrush and toothpaste, a comb, and a small mirror; but people took out their own money and bought me shirts, a towel and slippers. Almost overcome with emotion, I thanked them all. They told me they would get permission to visit me wherever I was held. I thanked them again and waved goodbye as we left the marketplace.

We returned to the bishop's house, and that afternoon I received the first visitors. The colonel ordered his guards to allow in anyone to visit "the Father." I was surprised by this liberality. Later I would understand the reason. The first group was made up of the "pillars" of the Makeni Church: three catechists; the chairman of the Pastoral Parish Council; and the old patriarch of the parish, Sir Joseph Golo-Musa. I received them at the gate of the compound to make sure that the guards did not give them a hard time. The authorities allowed me to take the visitors up to my room. There we sat down; some on the chairs, some on the bed. They were all enthusiastic about seeing me.

Golo-Musa spoke for all of them, saying that just yesterday they had finished the fifth novena. They had prayed in the cathedral every morning and evening for the last 45 days, entreating God, through the intercession of the Blessed Mother, that at least one priest be sent to them before Ash Wednesday. All the priests, the bishop, and the sisters were forced to flee the town two months earlier, just before the invasion.

"We received the answer to our first request," Sir Golo-Musa said. "You are here! Now we will continue to pray more novenas so that we can obtain peace." They asked me to bless the ashes on Wednesday and celebrate holy Mass in the cathedral. I told them that I would be delighted to do so, but first they had to obtain permission from the authorities and get me some vestments, hosts, and wine. They told me they had all these things, although they had had some problem finding the wine. Some of the vestments had been spared from the pillage in the cathedral church and could be used. My guests asked me if I needed anything else for my comfort. I told them I had everything essential, but if they could provide me with one pillow, one volume of the Breviary (one of the four books containing the Divine Office, the official daily prayers of the Church that priests offer every day throughout the year), and some toilet tissue, I would be very grateful. They promised to get these from the abandoned Mission's buildings, where, following the withdrawal of the missionaries and repeated rebels' forays, whatever was left lay scattered.

My visitors told me of their sufferings —the deaths (both by killings and sickness), the deprivation and the molestation they had endured for the last two months since the withdrawal of the ECOMOG forces and the invasion of the rebels. I cried with them. When they had exhausted everything they had to say to me, I began asking about some specific news I was eager to know. Were any of the priests around? Any damage to the cathedral? To the hospital? What about the Sisters of Mother Teresa of Calcutta? Two hours passed easily. It was late in the afternoon, so the five visitors took leave by asking for my blessing, which I gave as they knelt. Again, I fought back a surge of emotion. Just as they departed, one furtively thrust something into my hand; it was money. I whispered "thank you." Any other words refused to come out of my throat.

Shortly after their departure, a child came in, smiling, with a bowl of rice and sauce. She said, "I am Fatmata, and this is for you, Father." I thanked her, returning her smile and patting her on the cheek. I said, "Fatmata, come back soon to collect the bowl, and there will be some left for you." She scurried away with a giggle.

A few minutes later, an orderly knocked on my door. "There is another visitor for you."

"Fine, let him come in," I said. A young woman entered, rosary in one hand and a small plastic bag in the other. "I am Cecilia. I have come to see you, Father, and to find out how you are and whether you need anything."

"Sit down, Cecilia. Thank you for coming. I am happy to see you." "

"This is for you, Father," she said, holding out the plastic bag, "Here are some oranges and bananas." She told me how sorry she was to see me in detention. She inquired about what they were giving me to eat and volunteered to bring me a flask so I could keep water hot and make coffee or tea. I learned that she was a college student at Port-Loko Teachers College. She lived in Congo Town (a suburb of Makeni) and was a friend of all the priests in that Mission, in particular Father Gizzo.

Cecilia asked me to pray for her and for Sierra Leone, for she very much feared what was going on in the country. I asked, "Aren't you risking too much by coming to visit me?" She answered, "Yes, but I know the first wife of the colonel well, and therefore no one would dare molest me." Even so, she was afraid. Seeing her willingness to help me, I asked if she could buy me some instant coffee, some powdered milk, sugar, and biscuits. I gave her the fifteen thousand Leones I'd just received. Before leaving, the girl dropped to her knees and asked for my blessing. I blessed her, said goodbye, and watched her leave, grateful for her visit.

Evening set in. In spite of all the visiting and attention I'd received, I felt somewhat depressed. The music was blaring full blast. I decided to go out into the compound as far as possible from the house to seek relief from the music and to pray the Rosary. Behind and at some distance from the bishop's house there was a grotto, a re-creation of the grotto of the apparitions of the Blessed Mother at Massabielle near Lourdes. I explored behind it to get away from all the eyes watching me. Behind the grotto I found a narrow space before reaching the chain-link fence running alongside the limits of the property. I settled there to pray. Since I had no Breviary, the Rosary was the only formal, vocal prayer I could offer. After a short time I noticed eyes peeking at me from the sides of the grotto. Guards were watching closely lest I escape. Seeing that I was praying, they left me alone; but a couple of them sat nearby with guns in their hands.

After a while I returned to the house. It was dark. The music had subsided, and I enjoyed a few moments of respite. As I sat in my room, I heard a knock at the door. Four young ladies came in. who occupied the room in front of mine. They were all smiles. "Father," they said, "We have come to cheer you up." Without further ado, they began singing a lively religious song, accompanying their singing by a light dance. They brought a smile to my face, and that reinforced their effort. Soon they formed a circle around my chair. The singing over, they introduced themselves as Agnes, Isatu, Kadiatu, and Gbinty. They were between 15 and 24, and had very pleasant dispositions. All had been abducted like me and now served the warriors as wives or companions. Their giggling was soon overcome by a new wave of earsplitting music that prompted them to leave my room at a dancing pace.

It was about 9 p.m. I was tired, hot and wanted to sleep. It was hot. I removed my trousers and T-shirt and lay down on the bed. It was comfortable, but how could I sleep with the music blasting away? All of a sudden the door flew open. Three children burst in, laughing. Seeing me in bed, they disappeared as fast as they had come. I got up and locked the door. So much for sleeping. I took a book from the many lying on the floor. Thank God it was an interesting novel, *Lazarus* by Morris West.

Time passed. 11 p.m., midnight, 1 a.m., 2 a.m.—the music continued. Around 3:30 a.m. mercifully the loudspeakers fell silent. Thanks be to God. I dropped onto my bed and fell asleep, but only briefly. A burst of gunfire not far from my window awakened me. I heard shouts and excited commands in Mende (the tribal language most commonly spoken by the RUF). Then quiet, only to be followed in a few minutes by animated talk just outside my window. It went on and on. Night guards sitting underneath my window were killing time. Oh, God, when would I be able to sleep? Finally, at around 4 a.m. I conked out.

General Routine of Subsequent Days:
The Atmosphere

It did not strike me the Sunday afternoon I arrived in Makeni. Not even the first night. I guess that the overpowering disco music absorbed most of my attention. Another reason may have been that the hustle and bustle of recent events had dulled me to the point that I had become immune to further stimuli. But I noticed it that morning – shooting! Constant, if intermittent, shooting of various kinds of weapons was going on: from light pistols to automatic rifles; heavy staccato shots of multiple rocket launchers, thunderous explosions of cannon balls or hand grenades. Always shooting, day and night, and we were not in the actual war front.

Upon my inquiry as to the reasons for this shooting, I was told that new or repaired weapons needed to be tested all the time and that the fighters had to practice as often as possible, so as not to lose their fighting readiness. That was the official version. I am sure that some sort of testing was going on in various areas. However, I also discovered through personal witness that a lot of these young warriors were trigger-happy and—particularly when they were more heavily under the influence of alcohol, drugs, or both—they would shoot just for kicks. Then again, there was shooting because of infighting, over petty arguments, money or women. Be that as it may, the end result was always the same: frightening noise 24 hours of the day, creating an atmosphere of threat, insecurity and foreboding.

From the very first moment of my abduction, my hope was that I would be allowed to go back to my Mission post. I said this to everyone around me, as often as I could, even publicly and directly to the higher command of the RUF. My questions were always the same: "What good am I to you here? What do you hope to achieve by holding me? In fact, by your capturing and holding me, you are hurting your own cause. While I am here with you I can do nothing for you and my capture will only be viewed as a further confirmation of the bad image you have created with the general population. On the other hand, if you let me go, you will have a valid voice in Freetown to put forward your own quest for justice and peace, which I have always agreed with, although, as a man of God, I can never justify your methods and your warfare."

So went my reasoning with them, and I believe that most of them were in agreement with me, so much so that both the common young warriors as well as higher-ups such as captains, majors, and even some colonels responded that I should be patient and that they would release me in a short time. It was with this understanding and hope that I lived from day to day. Yet, as time passed, I began to suspect that the very highest level of the RUF authorities in Makeni were not of the same mind. This caused me to renew and intensify my prayer all day long. I prayed from morning to night and from night to morning. God truly became my refuge.

People near me generally respected me and, within certain limits, heeded my occasional small requests. Officers in the higher echelon kept aloof, however, and were cold and even threatening. Over 50 people lived in the bishop's house. This included the colonel, his two wives and children, several lieutenants, sergeants, ordinary rebels, a dozen child soldiers, and an indeterminate number of young women, varying from day to day but regularly numbering at least 15 or 20.

The large house—the six original bedrooms, the bishop's chapel, the living room, and the conference room—was converted into small dormitories with three, four, or more persons in each. There was no room reserved for dining. According to the African custom, when the food was ready, each person ate alone in his or her own time and at any convenient place. I was the only one with a room to myself, including a shower, which, however, could not be utilized as such, since the running water had been cut off. The good thing was that the shower could be used as a bath stall. Children and women brought me two buckets of water per day (most days).

On the grounds, scattered within the fenced area around the house and all the way to the main gate, there were bed-size foam rubber pads (looted from stores in town) for the rebels on duty to lie down as they kept watch day and night. During the dry season no rain would be expected for months on end. The heat was always stifling, even at night. Malaria-infected mosquitoes were a threat.

Surrounding the bishop's house outside the fenced-in area, another 60 or so young rebels with other officers, including captains and lieutenants, lived in half a dozen smaller confiscated houses.

There was some kind of discipline in rebel camps, at least in those I have seen. It was routine for the commander at a given hour of the day, to assemble the group of young guerrillas and punish those who had infringed on the rules. This was paradoxical in that the infringements of the accused individuals were the very same as those perpetrated by the rebels as a group, only on a larger scale. It was preposterous because the discipline purported to uphold a system of justice, which was violated in the very act of advocating it.

Typically, the commander would call out a culprit and spell out the accusation. Perhaps 30 seconds, at most one minute, were granted to the accused for self-defense. In fact, most of the time he was not allowed to finish his defense. The commander then ordered an officer of lower rank to proceed with the stripping and tying up of the culprit for a public flogging by rope, stick or belt. Then came the flogging. A specified number of strokes were given; normally 10, sometimes 20, 50, or even 100 for major offenses involving loss of life, violation of women, or large amounts of stolen money. The exercise usually caused soul-wrenching screams, evoked heart-rending pleas to stop and extracted confessions, and promises of amendment offered in the hope that the punishment would be suspended. All this served no purpose, even when blood spurted freely. Once the punishment was complete, the disgraced and disgruntled victim would walk away sore and sulking, frequently accompanied by the laughter of his companions. This last reaction of the comrades-in-arms was something so distasteful that I still find hard to believe and understand, and even harder to justify. I think it may have something to do with a negative aspect of the otherwise beautiful African culture.

After the roll call, everyone scattered to tend to his or her duties. The music would start again and carry on until some palavers or altercations would arise, which was rather often, even a daily occurrence. The shouts, the accusations, the counter-accusations, the insults, and the cursing would either stop or drown out the music. I made it a point never to mix with the rebels in anything. I always greeted them with a smile but steered clear of their company, unless they themselves approached me, individually or as a group, to converse, ask questions or simply chat.

With the boiled water that Cecilia brought me every day, I made coffee or tea and allowed the remaining water to cool for use as drinking water during the day. Another girl agreed to do my laundry.

After my morning coffee, I would take a prayer book or the Breviary (when eventually it was made available to me) and go out in the compound, picking a place as far and as secluded as possible to protect myself from the stares of onlookers and the loud music. I paced up and down, praying the Psalms and other Scripture from the Breviary. After that I continued praying the Rosary, usually all 15 decades. (The Luminous Mysteries that brought the complete Rosary to 20 decades had not been introduced yet). Then I continued with the Marian litanies.

By approximately 10 a.m. I would pick a book from among the hundreds from the bishop's personal library, which were scattered all over the house and the compound and read until 1 or 2 p.m. My readings included theology, missionary strategies such as enculturation, and Xaverian history. After I tired of reading serious and deep material, I read novels. A wonderful lady named Janice England, a young volunteer of the Lay Mission Helpers of the Los Angeles Archdiocese, had left these behind for the bishop when, upon completing her tour of duty, she returned to the U.S. By around 3 p.m. the simmering heat caused me to lie down on the bed for a rest. Outside the house the heat was even more intense than inside. I would lie down, but I couldn't sleep on account of the heat and the loud music always thumping in my ears.

By four in the afternoon I would get up and again seek shelter in the compound as far away as possible from the music and the heat. I prayed some other parts of the Divine Office and then 15 more decades of the Rosary. By mid or late afternoon visitors would begin to come and enliven my day. At around 6 p.m. little Fatmata would bring me my bowl of rice with sauce. By then, 24 hours since my last meal, I felt hungry, but often my appetite would vanish while sitting on my chair, in the oven that was my room, thinking of the lack of hygiene in preparing the food.

I oftentimes witnessed the cooking process and was revolted—not by the quality and kind of the African food, which I always liked and enjoyed—but on account of the utter lack of cleanliness of the cooking implements and the wandering of goats, chickens, and dogs around the plates of food lying on the ground during the dishing out. Given these circumstances, I often tried to swallow a few mouthfuls of rice and wash it down with lukewarm water. The water itself tasted like kitchen grease. It was usually boiled in a kitchen pot and had acquired the flavor of burned palm oil. Thank God I could refresh my mouth with some fruit, such as oranges or limes, brought by visitors and friends.

After dinner I would continue to spend time with visitors or return to my prayers, the Divine Office in the Breviary and 15 more decades of the Rosary as circumstances dictated. Visits of my people (boys, men, girls, and women, mostly parishioners of Makeni) were always heartening experiences that lifted up my often low spirits. These true Christians braved the danger of being harassed and even molested, as well as the hardship of having to walk some two miles in the tropical heat to bring me all sorts of things: fruit, cakes, soft drinks, clothes, and even money. And they themselves were so desperately in need of the essentials to survive!

Between eight and nine o'clock, as darkness fell, and all visitors had left, I resumed praying: another 15 decades of the Rosary. Sometimes I would sing to myself, under my breath, hymns and songs until I was ready to settle down into bed. To sleep? No. Deafening music and sporadic shooting kept me company until the wee hours of the morning, when I would finally be overcome by sleep.

I titled this section "routine," but it should be understood that it was routine only when other events did not interfere. As I was writing these memoirs, it occurred to me that routine was, perhaps, a misnomer and unexpected events should have been labeled "routine."

Brainwashing: *Their Philosophy*

One of the more frequent unscheduled activities was rebels lecturing to me by direct discourse or rhetorical questioning, either in formal sessions or just in passing. Mostly in long discourses they tried to convince me of the goodness of their revolution, the "movement," as they called it. According to them, their Movement was totally misunderstood by many of the people of Sierra Leone, but nevertheless it was a necessary event to correct the many evils in the country that had been going on since its independence and even before. I never instigated these explanations because the rebels' claim to be the saviors of a country enmeshed in total corruption was so common and so distorted vis-à-vis the political reality that I felt it useless to argue. So I was merely a recipient of their lectures. Briefly, this was the scenario given to me by the young theoretician Abdul Richardson-Kamara:

"The political world of Sierra Leone has become so corrupt that its leaders, from the start of our independence, have one after the other sodomized and prostituted our country for their own pleasure and lust for power. They have constantly taken from the public and from individuals any benefit they could. Furthermore, these bad leaders, for their own personal gain, have allowed foreigners to exploit and rob our resources to the point that Sierra Leone had become the poorest country in the world, at the very bottom in the list of developing countries compiled by the United Nations. These politicians have provided such an enticing example of greed and selfishness that the common citizen too has become corrupt, even in his own private life, thus contributing to the misery of our society. In this atmosphere of despair, God unleashed the fury of the revolution. Our movement has come, in the words of Ezekiel (7:1–27), to destroy and uproot all things and all people. Then out of the suffering and the destruction of all, a new order and a new society will arise, bringing Sierra Leone to her honorable place among the nations of the world, where God meant her to be. So whatever is happening now is God's work, and we are his agents. Our last operation coded 'No Living Thing' is the best example of the first part of our mission: to destroy all people, even the villagers who have supported the corruption, and uproot all things."

I heard this interpretation of Abdul, at least in part, from several other rebels. However, it cannot be said that all fighters accepted this interpretation of the movement. There certainly were as many rationales for the revolution, perhaps even less philosophical and more mundane, as there were rebels or leaders in it. It is relatively easy to inflame the spirits and to create rationales of vindication when people are suffering from any number of reasons, especially from true or even imaginary injustices.

One potent factor in this rebel war was the possession of diamonds. Sierra Leone is a country rich in alluvial diamond, considered by the experts in the business as being uniquely beautiful and therefore very highly priced in the world market. Charles Taylor, the president of Liberia and one of the instigators and mentors of the civil war in Sierra Leone, became the principal outlet for these diamonds. While these precious stones can be found in many rivers all over the country, they are highly concentrated in the Kono area. The rebels converged their first efforts and fought their fiercest battles to conquer the diamond fields of Kono. Diamonds then became their primary financial source for purchasing weapons, hence the appellation "blood diamonds." The United Nations banned the marketing of them. How far the fever for blood diamonds influenced the war and contributed to the corruption of the rebels, especially the leaders, is difficult to determine.

It must be admitted that Sierra Leoneans have been cruelly suffering for a very long time from real corruption and other factors. Unfortunately, however, the rebels' solution proved far worse and afflicted a greater number of individuals and the country as a whole far more than any evil in existence before their revolution. This became abundantly clear during the nine months the rebels actually governed Sierra Leone before being dislodged by the ECOMOG peacekeeping forces of West Africa.

The rebels proclaimed their concepts over and over to me, sometimes stressing one part over another. They would describe at length how the various foreign powers depleted Sierra Leone's natural resources. Also they would point out the supposed or real neglect we missionaries had demonstrated, when, they claimed, we failed to denounce such exploitation, as well as other injustices. The rebels would describe the real or supposed wickedness of the various political leaders and say that while the government and the world accused the RUF of atrocities, it was actually the SL government itself, the Nigerians of ECOMOG, or the Kamajors (the Mende hunters organized into a Civil Defense Force against the RUF) who were really responsible for these atrocities. In reality some atrocities were committed by renegade Sierra Leone soldiers and the Kamajors.

Finally, the rebels declared that wherever they themselves established their own rule, things were fine. People were happy and grateful. In this context, several times they proposed that if I agreed to stay in Makeni willingly and minister to the people, they would free me immediately. In fact, if I agreed to minister to the rebels themselves as a chaplain, they would make me an officer with the rank of captain or major!

This proposal helped me understand why the rebels so willingly accepted the request of the parishioners that I celebrate Mass in the cathedral church and administer the sacraments to the people. Of course, I pointed out in polite but unequivocal terms that it was they who took me by force and kept me there against my will. I told them that just as they had a general I too had a "general," the bishop, and only he could assign me (or deploy me to use their military jargon) to Makeni and/or to serve as a priest for the rebels. Only then would I accept their offer.

This position I made clear, even in public, while preaching in the cathedral in front of a packed church, including many rebels and some in high command. It may have been my unyielding position that strengthened their determination to hold me. In fact, some of the colonels said, *"He must stay with us until the very end. Let him be a witness to the things that are happening here. The bishop never paid any attention to us. They always snubbed us by running from us. Let them see what they have contributed to. Let him be here with us till this thing is resolved, and let him know that he'll be the first to die if things go wrong for us."*

Incidents: *"You Are a Mercenary"*

While studying the social sciences, I read about the socio-psychological notion of the *approval motive* as one of the most potent determinants of human behavior. This is the tendency of human beings, who naturally yearn to be liked and admired, to give a positive reason for their actions. Thus the approval motive can be applied to the rebels' behavior in my case. They had to justify my detention to make them look good to themselves and the world.

One night at about 1 a.m. Brigadier General Jussu Kamara, the 25-year-old commanding officer of the RUF in Makeni, summoned me to a marathon interrogation session in front of a few big names of the movement. He charged: "This white man, this supposed missionary priest, is not a man of God, but rather a belligerent agent against our struggle." Those around me were drinking hard liquor, and smoking marijuana or something like it. I was offered a Coke by one of the girls, and I gratefully accepted it. The brigadier general was launching into his harangue, trying to prove my collaboration with the Kamajors (the Civil Defense Forces allied to the government) as a foreign mercenary.

At one point I tried to protest. "Brigadier General, sir. I beg leave to talk. Where are these proofs that I am a mercenary and a trainer of the Civil Defense Force?"

"Ah!" he said with an air of triumph. "We have photos of you. We found military uniforms in your room. We found weapons. We have all these proofs."

I ventured, "Can I see these photos, please?"

"Here," he said. A small photo album was produced.

I recognized it immediately—photos taken 13 years earlier on a hunting trip through the Loma rain forest with a visiting group of Italian friends. The most incriminating photo showed me in a camouflage jacket and slacks, holding a shotgun, surrounded by four white men dressed in sport clothes. Then my beard was mostly black, whereas now it was snow white. Smiling, I explained that those photos were snapped while visiting with friends on a hunting trip a good eight years before the revolution even began.

"And the weapons we found in your room?" he pressed.

"General, sir," I said. "You are a guerrilla fighter. You must know that you don't go into battle with a museum piece like the big handgun that your people must have found in my room. It was an old Chinese gun, single shot, one foot long, the breech of which was so rusted, corroded, and jammed that it could never properly function again. It was a curiosity. The only other gun in my room was a 12-gauge single barrel shotgun—the very one appearing in the photo you are holding—which is quite good for shooting bush fowls or partridges, but certainly not to fight a war.

"As for the military uniforms you're talking about, it was only one, and it was a jacket worn while stalking game in a forest on hunting trips. Oh, yes. I had a hunting vest with shotgun cartridge pockets, hardly suited to hold rifle ammunition. You can rest assured, General, I am not and have never been a man of war."

This was the longest speech they ever allowed me to make during the 56 days I was held captive, except for my sermons in the cathedral. I think that the general's retinue were intrigued by my explanation, but then they started all over again repeating the same charges as if I had offered no explanation at all. I couldn't tell if they were under the influence of alcohol or drugs or both. At any rate, it was abundantly clear that they wanted to have the floor, so I let them have it.

Among the members of the interrogation panel there was one elderly gentleman, clearly not a military man, who was visibly anxious to address me, but was never given a chance by the others in the group. Having determined that it was useless to respond to the avalanche of talk going on, which shifted from accusations to deprecations, from vindications to self-exaltations, from their super-prowess and cleverness to their military strengths, I sat there with a smile, nodding approval or disapproval as the case required, but without uttering or even attempting to utter a single word.

Eventually the harangue ebbed out. The general used the pretext of someone addressing or calling him from behind me and left the room. It was already 2 a.m. and I wished I could lie down. The panel's talking became confused; they were all speaking at once. Finally, the elderly gentleman became bold and leaned over and introduced himself. He had been the Minister of Education in the AFRC (Armed Forces Revolutionary Council) government brought in by the coup of J.P. Koroma, in cahoots with the rebels, a government that was eventually overthrown by the ECOMOG forces after less than a year of spasmodic life. These forces were successful in reestablishing the legitimate government of President Tijan Kabba.

The old gentleman, whose name escapes me, stated that he was a Catholic, brought up by the Holy Ghost Fathers in the Eastern Province, but academically self-taught. He declared that he didn't like the missionaries because they wanted to impose their own Western culture on Sierra Leone. I felt better about the new topic and in spite of the late hour gave him eager attention. I readily agreed with him that missionaries who tried to impose their culture were certainly wrong. As usual, I was not allowed to expatiate much because he plunged on, like a ship in full sail. I quickly realized that while his main premise of condemnation was quite correct his understanding of culture itself (the minor premise) was debatable. I was confirmed in my assessment when he confronted me with the following question: "When the missionaries forbade us to worship our Nomolies (these are soft stone sculptured images of the ancestors, usually buried in the tomb of the dead – an integral part of Animist religions), what do you think? Do you think you white men have the right to interfere with our traditions and culture?"

His question was clear and direct. I was glad he used the

term "worship" because it brought up the weakest (theologically) side of his challenge. So I turned the question back to him. "What do you think?" I asked. "You tell me that you are a Christian and have been brought up as a Christian. What do you, as a Christian, think about worshipping the Nomolies?" He smiled without answering. By now all members of the party had left the room of the interrogation and had joined the music, the drinking and carousing. I took the excuse that I needed to go to the bathroom and disappeared. It was 3:30 a.m.

A Night of Terror

The extraordinary unity the RUF showed in battle was even more surprising when considering the discord in their camps. I found that internal differences of all kinds were commonplace. Quarrels and brawls were a daily occurrence and at times these put my life in jeopardy. The following event serves as an example.

It happened on Sunday night, March 21, at the bishop's house, where there were 100 or more warriors. It was 9:15 p.m., pitch dark and a moonless night. I was finishing my last Rosary at the grotto, after which I would retire to my room.

Three or four single shots from heavy rifles like AK-47s, immediately followed by helter-skelter running and shouting, shattered my meditation. Then more shouting, and orders. "Stop!" Screams. Shots from smaller automatic weapons.

In utter darkness I felt my way to the house as quickly as possible. I didn't know what was going on, but inside I would at least be out of the range of bullets, whether stray or aimed. Not wanting to draw attention by using the flashlight inside the darkened house, I felt my way to the stairway. I climbed the stairs and I locked myself in my room. Outside, the shooting, shouting, and screaming went on. I couldn't figure out what was happening. Then I heard a light, but insistent, knock at my door. I opened it and saw Gloria, the colonel's youngest wife, holding her three-week-old baby. She asked, "Father, what is going on? May I come into your room? I am afraid."

"Come in, come in," I said, quickly closing the door behind her. "You're asking me what's going on? You live here. I'd like to ask you what's going on. Are these your men?"

Gloria came in and sat on the bed saying, "No. They are not our men. Someone is attacking us."

I went to the window and peeked out. In the darkness I could only see flashing sparks from rifles and the rapid arrow-like movements that were tracer bullets. Suddenly there was heavy stomping up the stairs and the bashing-in of doors. Then strange steps, things being shuffled or dragged around, but no voices. Curiosity got the best of me. I slowly opened the door and stole a look. In the dark corridor I saw fast-moving shadows silhouetted on and off by flashlights. People were moving in and out of adjacent rooms, dragging things: beds, mattresses, radios, and chairs.

I quickly pulled my head in, softly shutting and locking the door. "They are taking everything. Who are they?" I asked.

The din outside continued. There was a heavy rap on the door. I opened it quickly, knowing well that any delay would make the intruders break it down. A flash of light hit my eyes. A voice in the darkness asked, "Who is here? Who are you?" "I am Father Victor, a priest."

"Oh, you are the priest? Stay here. Don't worry. Nothing will happen to you. Just stay in." He shut the door and left. Gloria was shivering behind me. "Let's pray," she suggested. "Okay," I replied. "Let's start the Holy Rosary."

More raps at the door. I quickly opened it again and was blinded by a bright beam again. A rough voice commanded, "Who are you? Come out, you two, come out and get in line." Someone grabbed me by the shirt and dragged me out, felt my wrists, pulled off my watch, and ordered me to line up with the others down below. "Hurry, hurry. Follow me," he said.

The confusion and noise rose to a crescendo. Just as we reached the ground floor the young rebel turned right, heading to the west exit of the house. Gloria, holding her baby, elbowed me, beckoning me to turn to the left for the east exit. "Let's run," she whispered.

We rushed through the east door and ran toward the grotto. On the right side of the grotto, flush with the ground, there was an almost invisible slit in the chain-link fence. I had detected it days before while praying the Rosary there and looking for escape routes. Swiftly and wordlessly I lay down parallel to the slit of the fence and rolled under it to the other side. I quickly got up and lifted the lower edge of the wire mesh as high as possible so that Gloria could hand me her baby. Then she too followed my example, lay down, and rolled under the fence. Together we ran into the thick woods, feeling our way behind the bishop's house, away from all the turmoil.

I was looking for a path that I knew should be there, but I couldn't find it. I dove through the thick brush with the weight of my entire body, stamping down the thorn bushes under my feet. Thank God for my leather boots. I was trying to move away as fast as possible while at the same time making a path for Gloria and her baby. Finally, after 10 yards or so, we came to a clearing and took a deep breath. No one followed us. I doubted that the rebel leading us out of the house had discovered we weren't with him until he emerged from it on the opposite side.

The darkness, the chaos, the thundering explosions, all that had created such a threatening atmosphere just moments before, were now protecting us. We kept moving, distancing ourselves from the mayhem. The roar became noise, then distant sound, punctuated by muffled explosions and faint shouting. Thank God it was the dry season, no danger of rain. Gloria took the lead. Native Africans have far better night vision and a better sense of orientation than most of us Europeans or Americans. Holding her baby tight, she led me by a wide semicircle around the bishop's compound toward Congo Town, a locality adjacent to Makeni. She skillfully picked her way around invisible obstacles, swiftly and silently moving like a shadow.

It must have been 11 p.m. Here and there we could see candles or lights and the shapes of huts and houses. As we approached some of the entrances, people furtively gathered around and whispered questions to Gloria. She took me to a large house with lots of people around it. I learned later that it was the home of a good Catholic family.

Mr. Williams, the head of the family, said, "Come in, Father, come in. Sorry for what is happening. Come in and lie down." Holding a kerosene lantern, he guided me into a room where there was a nice bed, apparently untouched. "Please, Father, lie down. Teresa will go and fetch you some water." I thanked him profusely and sat on the bed. Teresa, who must have been about 18, came in with a tray holding a pitcher of cold water, a glass, and some biscuits. "How sweet of you. Thank you," I whispered.

Louise Williams, the mother, entered the room and reassured me. "Don't worry about anything, Father." I asked about Gloria. "She's all right, Father. She's with the girls and the baby in the other room. Relax, Father, you are safe here."

After the mother and the girl left, I stretched out on the bed. Only faraway sounds and nearby hushed voices reached me now. It took a long time before I could sleep—one hour, perhaps two. It was hard to tell without a watch. Mercifully, I finally fell asleep.

Soft singing of children mixed with adult voices awakened me. I listened. The mother was leading her children in morning prayers. How beautiful they sounded. I dragged myself out of bed. Light was filtering through the window. I arranged my hair with my hand and walked out.

On the veranda I found three beautiful children—a young boy and two teenage girls—and their mother. I joined in prayer, if not by singing, at least in spirit. They greeted me with a smile and offered me a chair. They came and went in their religious singing, tidying themselves up and attending to small chores. Eventually they brought me a bowl of water and a towel, as well as coffee and biscuits. What a happy family! How could they live so, on the edge of a war? But I discovered that they were not just on the edge when Mr. Solomon rolled up his sleeves to show me livid bruises on both his arms. Only two weeks earlier rebels had tied him up and dangled him from the branch of a tree for three days, threatening to kill him if he did not surrender something the rebels were looking for, but which he did not have. Louise told me of the danger they lived in, particularly for their two daughters.

By now people began to congregate from many sides. Gloria, smiling, came to the veranda with her baby. Still, nobody knew what had happened last night. Finally, Captain Steven, an officer under the colonel, came and told us part of the story, at least the part he himself was able to figure out.

Brigadier General James sent a detachment of RUF rebels, under another supposed colonel, to arrest Colonel Tony. They tied up Colonel Tony and a number of his commandos. They beat them up and wounded the colonel, along with several others. Captain Steven eventually saved the situation by shooting an RPG (rocket-propelled grenade) in the air over the mayhem. The loud explosion scared the attackers and put them to flight; however, most of the things were already looted from the main house.

Captain Steven told us that we should now return to the bishop's house. Later I learned from other sources an additional element of the story: Colonel Tony was reportedly abusing some civilians in town who had connections higher up, and this resulted in punitive action against him. Whether this attack at the bishop's house had been properly authorized or not, we will never know.

This incident was just one of several similar episodes, some more serious, which took place at Makeni in the first four months of 1999. Looted from the bishop's house were also the few things good people had brought me—the Breviary book of the Divine Office, the towel, the flask, Lt. Jacob's small radio, the mattress, the two shirts and the trousers. All these things would be replaced again, some for the second and third time, by the generosity of our Christians who again took from the little they had to help me. Though I'd lost everything again, there was also a bright side to this incident: the amplifier, the large speakers, and stereo player had also disappeared. Thanks be to God for sparing me that infernal music, at least for a time.

Operation "Rescue the Missionary"

We live in an age of ecumenism, but I would never have thought that during my detention by the RUF I would witness such a striking example of ecumenical cooperation as I did. Along with the exceptional sensitivity of good Catholic people regarding my health, well-being, and security while in rebel hands, a similar concern was shown by some people outside of our fold.

To achieve my liberation three Catholics—Sir Golo Musa, George Sesay, and James Tarawally—went to tremendous lengths; and three local ministers of other Christian denominations cooperated greatly. There also was a helper from the most unlikely quarters who coordinated, pushed, and maneuvered for the same purpose. He was an Islamic *Karamoko* (a title of reverence similar to "Monsignor" in the Catholic Church), a Muslim chaplain to the RUF with the rank of major. His name was Major Demba Mara of the Kuranko tribe.

Sir Golo Musa visited me every day. While he was very grateful to God for answering his prayers to provide a priest for the community of Makeni before Ash Wednesday, he also sympathized with my plight as a prisoner and prayed night and day for my deliverance.

Prior to the war, George Sesay had been one of my boys in the Catholic youth movement I had organized in Makeni when I was residing there. Later, he became a lecturer at the Makeni Teachers Training College. Major Demba Mara presently occupied (confiscated) George's house. In his clever way of doing things, George had befriended the Imam Karamoko and had brought my case to his attention.

Major Demba sent for me. After obtaining permission from Colonel Tony, George and I walked under escort some two miles to the compound of the major's house. It was filled with people: Sierra Leone soldiers (deserters), RUF warriors, civilian men, women and children. I was told that they all were there to have their arguments settled by the Karamoko. As we entered the main room, we found the major listening to a difficult case between a RUF rebel and a Sierra Leone soldier over the possession of a woman. On seeing me, the major excused himself from the assembly, came toward me, and, speaking in Krio, loudly and exuberantly greeted me: "Father! Come in, please!"

The major led me into a side room. I followed, accompanied by George, my RUF escorts, the major's attendant, and a translator because the Karamoko had reverted back to his Kuranko language. In the privacy of the room we sat on a large bed and Major Demba asked me what I would like him to do for me. I explained how I had been captured and taken away from my Mission post and how my absence was causing great harm not only to my work in the church and the schools, but also to many poor, sick and handicapped children who were depending on my care.

After listening, Major Demba told me that he had heard of the wonderful things we missionaries had been doing in the country and that he had always been very much against his people (the RUF) taking missionaries as hostages. He promised me that he would go all out to obtain my immediate release and that through his friend George, he would keep me informed.

I headed back to my prison in great elation and admiration for the wonderful disposition of this Muslim Karamoko "Brother." From that day on, George and his brother Moses kept me abreast of the efforts of the Karamoko with Brigadier General Jussu of the RUF, Brigadier General Thomas of the Sierra Leone Army, and General Bumpeh (a Liberian) of the RUF. Every day George walked miles under the scorching sun to tell me how Major Demba undertook measures to personally visit every big leader of the rebels in the Makeni area to persuade them to release me.

In the meantime, James Tarawally, a pillar of the church in Makeni, teamed up with Sir Golo Musa and a few of the other church leaders to lobby one or another of the commanding officers. However, as all these efforts were going on, it became increasingly evident to me that in spite of what the chief leaders might have said to the Karamoko and the others pushing for my release, they were not really willing to let me go.

Still, the efforts continued, and when it seemed to the Karamoko that all authorities were consulted and favorable to my release, there remained the problem of my transportation. He offered his own truck to carry me to the nearest Guinean entry border some 100 miles away, in the direction of Kamakwie, but for that he needed fuel. He then asked George to search and obtain 25 gallons of diesel. In that dry season fuel was scarcer than water in occupied Makeni. Gasoline and diesel prices had rocketed up to 50,000 Leones per gallon (equivalent to about $33.00 in U.S. currency) against 3,500 Leones in normal times.

Not easily discouraged, George, mostly on foot, scouted all of Makeni and even areas 25 miles away until he found the 25 gallons. He paid for part of it himself, but most he got on credit against his good name and reputation. Finding the fuel was only part of the difficulty. The next hurdle was to carry it to its destination. The Sierra Leone Army soldiers (deserters) and the RUF rebels were desperate for fuel. In addition, it was an illegal commodity for civilians to possess. The only way to transport diesel was to travel either by night or on back roads through the forest. The consequence of meeting a rebel while carrying the fuel was not only losing the whole lot, but could also be a bad flogging. This was the risk George undertook for my sake—for 15 days.

One day I approached Colonel Tony, who had always shown me some deference and yet had kept me under guard day and night at the bishop's house, and asked him kindly to follow me to my room. Having seated him comfortably in the only easy chair, I grabbed a straight chair, sat astride on it in front of him and asked pointblank: "Colonel, are you with me or against me?" He was surprised and stared at me, expecting an explanation for this question.

"Almost every day," I continued, "you tell me that I will be released soon, very soon. But it is now one month and a half and you keep repeating the same refrain with no consequence. How soon is soon?"

He replied, "Well, Father, it really is not up to me. Your case is in the hands of Brigadier Jussu."

"But," I pressed on, "you are a very close friend of the brigadier. Have you talked to him about me?"

He rejoined, "Yes, I have, but it is not easy. I will try again."

Two days later I decided to see Colonel Tony in his own office at the Logistics headquarters of the RUF in the center of Makeni. He was eating lunch with several other colonels, among whom I recognized the Head of Intelligence Colonel John Jarbo, a Catholic. As I entered the office, Colonel Tony — without inviting me to sit down, leaving me standing alone — said half in jest to his colleagues, "Here is Father Victor. He is pressing for his release."

Instantly they all, angrily and aggressively, began throwing questions at me concerning the behavior of the missionaries, the white men, the bishops, and the Catholics. All were rhetorical questions because they never permitted me to answer. Loudest of them all was Colonel John Jarbo. With a high-pitched voice he commanded, "He must stay here. Let him see what is going on. Let him be a witness till the end. We will know what to do with him!" What an ugly and threatening scene! Sizing the situation, with a wave of my hand I withdrew in disgust saying, "Excuse me, gentlemen."

I left the Logistics Compound more and more convinced that those people were in no mood to release me in spite of all the words spoken to them on my behalf by the Karamoko and other personalities. It was then that I decided to secretly enlist the help of the two young Catholic men, long-standing friends, who had offered to lead me in an escape on foot. We would reach the Guinean border, 130 miles away (in the Kambia direction), walking only at night and through back paths in the forest.

CHAPTER FIVE

The Fight Over Liberation

With all the efforts to liberate me by so many well-meaning and dedicated people, it is surprising that my actual release finally came from the rebels themselves, although not those in Makeni. Earlier on, 15 days after my capture, I had been given false hopes when I heard on the radio that Corp. Foday Sankoh, the historical and undisputed leader of the rebel movement, had ordered his field commanders to release every civilian prisoner within 72 hours including "the priest." When I heard this, I thanked God. I would be released soon. But days passed and nothing happened.

About a week after the radio announcement one night (that seemed to be the time best suited for the rebels to operate) Brigadier General Jussu summoned me and said, "We have received orders to release you, but I don't think I want to release you yet, because you are not a real priest. You are a mercenary."

Another standing by the general added, "If they really want us to release you, we could let you go, but before you reached the border we would have you shot down and then blame the Guineans or the Kamajors. We have done that before. Nobody will ever know." I thought he was bluffing and discounted his threat.

Corp. Foday Sankoh had been taken prisoner by the Nigerians and later was handed over to the Sierra Leone government. While in prison he was persuaded to contact his followers by radio and satellite phone in a bid to arrange a ceasefire and create a platform for peace negotiations. If he succeeded in this effort, the president of the Republic promised him a reprieve from the death sentence already pronounced on him. That was why Foday Sankoh had ordered the release of all civilian prisoners. It was meant to be a good will gesture toward the government and an assurance that he was serious in his efforts.

The bishop of Makeni, Msgr. George Biguzzi, SX, was then residing in Freetown, having fled Makeni at the time of the rebel attack. He was one of the main facilitators of the peace negotiations between the government and the RUF and as such, had access to Foday Sankoh in prison. Shrewdly, the bishop used his position to suggest to Foday Sankoh that his orders as commander in chief had no weight with his followers. How else could he explain that Father Victor Mosele was still being held a prisoner in Makeni a full month after Sankoh's specific instructions to release him within 72 hours?

Eventually the bishop's challenge, repeated over and over, sank in and became a nagging thought in the leader's mind.

This suspicion was reinforced by other real or apparent snubs by the Makeni group. Finally, Sankoh radioed or telephoned Brig. Gen. Dennis Mingo (whose battle name was Superman) to proceed from Lunsar, where he was stationed with his rebel troops, to Makeni, and arrest those who were defying his orders and set the priest free.

It was the night between Good Friday and Holy Saturday, April 3, 1999, 2:30 a.m. I was in my room, still wrestling with the oppressive heat of the night, when I heard a rumbling of engines accompanied by intense and sustained shooting. It was all coming from the west of the city, the direction of Lunsar and the capital, Freetown. Chaos and mayhem quickly spread through the bishop's house.

The shooting was from both big and small arms: rifles, machine guns, mortars and RPGs. In the house, the rebels began panicking. Everybody assumed that the long-expected invasion of Makeni by the ECOMOG forces to flush out the RUF had started. Colonel Tony was out of town, so Capt. Steven took charge and ordered the bishop's house to be evacuated of both women and children and the bulk of the guerrillas. The large and conspicuous building made for an easy target.

The rebels hid me in a small house in Congo Town village. Shooting continued and got closer, now from all directions, all through the rest of the night. As morning came, the shooting faded somewhat, but the tension, confusion and movement of fighters seemed to increase.

Finally, I was able to piece together enough bits of information from various sources to give me part of the picture. Eventually the captain himself confirmed to me that it was not the ECOMOG forces but Superman and a detachment of hundreds of his rebel warriors who came to attack Brig. Gen. Jussu's command. He had come to arrest some of the RUF leaders in town. Some were resisting, others were fleeing, including Brig. Gen. Jussu. Col. Rambo and other resisters had already been killed. Then Capt. Steven added: "Superman is looking for you, too! So stay hidden. Don't even come to the door or window!"

I needed no further prompting. The captain did not tell me, perhaps because he himself didn't know, that Superman sought me in order to set me free. On the other hand I knew of Superman's frightening notoriety from hearsay and eyewitnesses. I said to myself, "I don't want to fall from the frying pan into the fire!" So I fully cooperated with Capt. Steven and my other captors and even refrained from looking out the window. At times, when rebel patrols came by the house, I was shoved under a bed. I spent Holy Saturday and the night of the Easter Vigil in that house, never really sleeping, following the various noises: shootings, erratic orders being shouted out, inexplicable commotions, shuffling of patrol parties, and so forth.

On Easter Sunday the shooting had died out, yet I was prevented from going to the cathedral to celebrate Holy Mass, which had been arranged earlier in the week. The excuse given was that it was too dangerous for me to be seen. Superman was now in command of Makeni, and he was searching for me. Actually the rebels who held me were still loyal to Brig. Gen. Jussu and were still looking after his interests, not Superman's. Fortunately Father Kargbo, a diocesan priest, who had been in hiding from the rebels in the Makeni area, was reassured and convinced by friends and parishioners to come to the cathedral to offer the Easter Sunday Mass in my place. I thanked God for that arrangement.

I turned to the captain and said, "The shooting is finished. No one really is looking for me, and anyway the fighters of Superman have already searched the bishop's house and I will be safe there. Let me return to it; I know all your guerrillas have already gone back there." I was anxious to leave the house in the village for another reason. The four young rebels posted to watch me were lustfully eyeing two young girls in that house. The captain agreed, thinking the danger for me was over. In the evening, when it was dark, he ordered the four fighters to escort me back to the bishop's house.

On Monday at 3 a.m., a solitary pickup truck rushed into the bishop's compound carrying 12 rebels. A machine gun was mounted on top of the cab. Fear swept over the compound, for they all believed that Superman had come to punish them for frustrating his search for me. All warriors scattered. Inside the bishop's house, women began wailing. One of Superman's rebels jumped from the pickup shouting, "Stop this crying, nobody move. Nobody worry. We have not come to harm anyone. We have only come to get the priest."

I heard these words from the second floor of the bishop's house. I sat still on my bed. I heard the men's footsteps as they entered the house and climbed up the stairs. They approached my room and without knocking pushed the door open and looked in.

"Are you the priest?"

"Yes."

"Well, come, hurry. Superman wants to see you."

I grabbed my plastic bag, which held a few personal belongings, and followed them down the stairs, out of the bishop's house and into the truck. We arrived at Superman's quarters at 3:30 a.m. The music was blaring. The rebels were drinking and smoking marijuana. They stood me in front of a man who was standing surrounded by several other rebels; he was neither smoking nor drinking.

"Do you know who I am?" he asked in a calm voice, so different from all the commotion around.

"No." I said. "I don't believe I have ever met you, but I suppose you are Superman. They told me he sent for me."

"Yes. I am Superman. Do you know why I am here?"

"No, but I heard you have come to settle scores with Brig. Gen. Jussu and some of the other rebels because of some argument among yourselves."

"No, no, no," he protested. "That is not the case. I have come to arrest them because they were disobeying orders, and I know also that they were detaining you, against the wish of our leader. Tomorrow I am going to put you on a truck and you can go wherever you wish. You are free." I thanked him profusely. That indeed was good news! Yet little did I know that my ordeal was far from over.

Superman then sat down and had a chair brought for me and engaged me in a rather lengthy conversation. In spite of the late hour and the third night in a row without proper sleep, I was quite eager to answer his questions since I was so elated at the news of my freedom. He wanted to know if his colleagues had mistreated me. I assured him that they had not. He further asked me what my impression of them was.

I told him clearly that I saw them very divided amongst themselves, often squabbling and fighting. I also told him that, even though I agreed with the many grievances the rebels had against the government, I could not justify the war and was exceedingly saddened by the way the war was being fought and by the atrocities committed against innocent civilians.

I added another point that I had observed and which disappointed me, namely, that many of the rebels were very hostile toward the white man in general, including the missionaries. (I had in mind Lt. Col. John Jarbo and his like.) Superman vehemently denied that the movement had any animosity toward the white man in general and certainly none

Top row: After his injury, Father Victor Mosele was transported some 20 miles to safety. *Second row (l)*: Another casualty of war: this man's arms were cut off by rebels. A boy must help with daily routines like buttoning his shirt. © 1999, *The Washington Post. Photo by Michel DuCille. Reprinted by permission. (r)*: The bishop of Makeni, George Biguzzi, SX, poses with two ex-rebels. The prelate was captured, harassed and robbed on several occasions by RUF rebels. *Third row (l)*: Father Victor, Anthony Rogers (who led the escape), and Father Franco Manganello rest at Bane Loko. *(r)*: Father Franco plays the foot-pedal organ at the church in Madina. *Unless indicated, all photos © Daniel Conteh.*

Top row (l): Father Victor is supported by villagers, posing at Laia (Port Loko District). *(r)*: Twins who lost their legs during the war smile innocently, unaware of the challenges that face those with handicaps in a developing country. *Second row (l)*: Paul Lala, the youngster who scoured the village for rebels on the night of the escape. *(r)*: The remains of the government hospital in Kambia. The facility, which once boasted 150 beds, two operating theatres, a pharmacy and nurses quarters, is now reduced to shambles. *Third row*: Father Victor and Father Franco at Bane Loko, surrounded by two Gbetties of the Civil Defense Force. *Unless indicated otherwise, all photos © Daniel Conteh.*

toward the missionaries. He added that if I had that impression, it must have been conveyed only by some individuals in the group. It did not represent the view of the movement.

As for the atrocities, he insisted that if they had indeed been perpetrated by some of the rebels, the leadership had never authorized them. They were the fruit of individuals acting on their own. He also indicated that not all the atrocities were the responsibility of the RUF. Soldiers too (both deserters and regular army), and the government's civil defense units, particularly the Kamajors, bore the same blame for many atrocities perpetrated on civilians. "But now," he concluded, "now we all want peace."

I concurred with him on the desire for peace and I confirmed that I personally had heard this desire expressed by very many of the RUF fighters and SLA soldiers (deserters) in Makeni.

"Make sure," he insisted, "that you tell the whole world that we of the RUF want peace."

I assured him that I would do exactly that. It was almost 5 a.m. The place had become quiet. Outside it was still pitch dark. I was put in a small room with a big bed in order to rest for a while. The bed was still warm from the previous occupant(s). After only a short while I fell asleep. It was a short and fitful sleep. Around 7:30 a.m. the place came alive again with the movement and the voices of hundreds of warriors tidying up. Although sleep was short, it did help to keep me from physically breaking down. I lay in bed until around 9:30. Then I got up and, as I stepped out of the room, I almost bumped into a middle-aged man, bare-chested, holding an infant in his arms. I excused myself for the near collision, and then I complimented the "father" on the beautiful baby he was holding.

He said, "He is not my son, but they gave him my name."

"Oh!" I exclaimed, "And what is your name?"

"My name is Superman."

I apologized for not recognizing him only a few hours after I had met him. My mind had not registered his features since I was so exhausted, in a place with poor lighting, and in shock from the fast happenings around me the day and night before. He understood my embarrassment and brushed it aside with a hearty laugh. He asked me where I wished to be released to. Since Freetown and Kambia were cut off by the fighting still going on, I chose as my deliverance point the border pass into Guinea called Madina-Oula, some 25 miles northwest of Kamaqwie.

Another reason for this choice of Madina-Oula was that the rebels had taken from me all my identification documents and so entry into Guinea was very risky. Guinean border guards were known to be very difficult with people without ID and even more so with a white man in wartime. Some mercenaries from Europe were known to be involved in the fighting. But fortunately for me I had been to that point of entry before on several occasions, arriving there from the Guinean side to pick up other missionaries who were escaping the rebels from Sierra Leone. I had met both the military and police authorities there and hoped that they would recognize my face.

Later that day Superman summoned Colonel Kumba (battle name Papezumba)—the same one who had taken me captive in Kambia 50 days earlier—and ordered him to take me to the Guinean border at Madina-Oula, northwest of Kamaqwie and about 110 miles away from Makeni.

At one point at least four governments, through their agents, were trying to negotiate my liberation with the RUF rebels. They included the CIA; the Vatican, through the apostolic nuncio residing then in Conakry, Guinea; the Sierra Leone government, through the mediation of Bishop George Biguzzi; and, finally the Italian Government.

The Italians got into action as a consequence of a petition with some 3,000 signatures collected from the Italian public by a campaign of my relatives and friends, prominent among them were Dr. and Mrs. Mario Sibona, residents in Rome. The impasse seemed to be the unwillingness of our Missionary Society to engage in any sort of exchange or compromise with the rebels. Our prearranged policy was never to negotiate with the rebels over captured missionaries.

CHAPTER SIX
Trip to Freedom

Three full days passed between the order to set me free, and freedom itself—only three days, yet long and full of anxieties. Anything could have happened and what transpired in those three days was enough to impress me for a lifetime and to make me wish for death several times over.

I was invited to board a double cabin Toyota Stout pickup. I recognized it to be one of those commandeered by the rebels from one of our Missions. The distance between Makeni and the Guinean border by way of Kamakwie was approximately 110 miles. This distance, usually covered in eight hours on the typical Sierra Leone dirt roads full of potholes and makeshift bridges, became a three-day journey.

There was no standard fuel available in town. It had long ago been used up. Instead of diesel fuel the RUF, with typical African ingenuity, discovered an expedient substitute: palm kernel oil. They crushed the hard shell of the seed of the palm, then boiled and filtered the resulting black liquid, and this became the new fuel. Although it did not produce the same power as the diesel and in the long run (not too long at that) it clogged up the engine and corroded parts, it did work.

Our truck was loaded down with ammunition and 29 RUF fighters. They were hanging off the vehicle like huge clusters of grapes on a vine. Men and boys, holding their rifles, sat on the hood, cab and roof. Even on the front windshield legs dangled down, making for poor visibility for the driver. With that kind of load I was surprised that the vehicle could move at all. But move it did, though at a snail's pace.

I sat in the middle seat of the back passenger section, squeezing in with three other people: two men and one woman. My knees were pulled up close to my chin in a fetal position. To survive eight hours like that would have been barely possible, but for three whole days? I thought for certain I would die before reaching Guinea. Fortunately (in this respect) the truck kept breaking down, which gave me the opportunity to disentangle from my position. Under all that weight something had to give and eventually all did, one part after another: brakes, radiator, transmission, tires, and finally power itself cut off.

As the truck crawled up a long, moderate hill, at the upper part of the ascent it suddenly lost all power. Having no brakes, it began to roll backwards. As soon as the rebels sensed danger all of them jumped off like a bunch of grasshoppers. As for me, I was trapped inside. At the last minute my three seat companions and the one in front managed to roll out. Penned in as I was, I had no such chance. The truck picked up speed backward, veered sharply to the right, somersaulted, and ended down at a 90-degree angle in the ravine.

The glass between the cab and the back bed shattered. Ammunition boxes of rifle cartridges, hand grenades and RPGs filled the cabin. I found myself pinned upside down inside the truck and under the ammunition! Thank God I was still alive and in one piece, though in a pitiful predicament and helplessly trapped. The rebels rushed to the rescue and slowly pulled me out. Breathless and in shock, I stumbled out of the wreck and sat on a stone, while everyone stared at me as if I were a ghost. The thought kept on occurring to me: I will surely die before I reach the border. An hour later, amazingly enough, we were back on the road.

For the almost 30 years I lived among African people, I have marveled at the miracle of their resourcefulness. In spite of poverty of means and a lack of technical expertise, there was no predicament they could not tackle and often resolve, sometimes so ingeniously that it defied my white man's imagination. The rebels pulled the truck out of the ravine and worked on it while talking and shouting. They recovered the battery which had flown out of the hood and rolled down the incline, pushed and pulled and . . . the vehicle was running again!

After two nights and three days, we arrived eight miles from the Guinean border. The rebels said, "Look, we don't want to go any farther because we know that at the border there are

Guinean soldiers and we have orders not to engage them in a shootout. From here you will have to proceed on foot and alone."

I saw no problem in that arrangement. I felt so elated to finally be free that without much ado I took off alone, waving goodbye to them as if they had been my greatest friends.

After I walked for about a half hour, suddenly the words came back to my mind, "Yes, we can let you go, but before you reach the Guinean border we'll shoot you down and blame the Guineans for it. Nobody will ever know." I broke out in cold sweat and shuddered. Worry became paramount and I almost slipped into paranoia. As I was walking through the narrow path of the forest, I kept looking front, back, and sideways, straining my eyes and ears to pick up any sign of danger, wondering. Always wondering! For three hours I walked alone under the scorching African sun. It was mid afternoon when I started walking through an unfamiliar, solitary and secluded place with that echo sounding in my ears. What anxiety! What a torment!

About a half a mile from the Guinean border I donned a white robe that I had taken from the bishop's house and stuffed into the plastic bag of my belongings the night they came to take me to Superman. Finally, as sunset was approaching, I was relieved and overwhelmed to see the border. Tired, disheveled and dirty, I reached the military post of the border.

The Guineans soldiers somehow had been informed through the international news of BBC and CNN that the missionary had been released three days earlier and was on his way to their border. When they saw the white robe, they immediately recognized me. In fact one of them remembered me from my previous dealings with them. They greeted me, took me in, fed me and gave me a towel and some water for bathing.

Under a tree in the center of the camp they set up for me an army cot to spend the night since darkness had already set in and the nearest town was Kindia, 32 miles away. They themselves lay down on cots in the open around a big fire. Under the shining stars I fell into a deep and peaceful sleep. It was April 9, 1999, exactly 56 days since my capture in Kambia on Feb. 12.

On the following day the Guineans soldiers took me by a military truck to their command post at Kindia. After meeting their commander and thanking him for rescuing me, I asked them to drop me off at a convent of Benedictine nuns in the area. The nuns knew me there because I had visited them when I had come to receive the missionaries running from Sierra Leone. They had been alerted of my release by the media. However, before reaching the good sisters' house I asked the soldiers to lead me to a marketplace to buy some basic items such as a pair of sandals, a set of underwear, a comb, and a handkerchief. I used the last of the money my Christian friends had given me in Sierra Leone, which I had hidden in my underwear for almost a month.

When I entered the Benedictine monastery, the sisters were surprised by my appearance. But once they recognized me, they overwhelmed me with attention and care. We went to their chapel to thank God for His grace; and then after some food we settled down to plan how I should get to Conakry, the capital city of Guinea. By the satellite telephone we got in touch with the Apostolic Nuncio, Archbishop Monsignor Antonio Lucibello. In spite of the long distance (almost a four-hour drive on paved roads) His Excellency personally came to meet me and take me to the Archbishop's house in Conakry. I was finally out of all the worries and dangers that had beset me for the past two months.

Thanks be to Almighty God and to all people of goodwill who contributed to my safety and liberation.

CHAPTER SEVEN

Interlude Between Two Captures

From the remarks of my relatives who came to meet me at the Malpensa airport of Milan, Italy, my looks must have been frightening. I was gaunt, jaundiced, somewhat unsteady, and so underweight that they thought I was wearing an oversized suit. They took me directly to our Motherhouse in Parma, where after a quick debriefing by my superiors, I received a thorough medical check-up. Initially there was suspicion of heart and liver problems. But, thankfully, these were only false alarms. All the diagnostic tests turned up negative, although the clinical lab report showed an almost total depletion of my lab values. It took two and a half months of therapy to bring my lab values, body color, and weight back to normal. Much love and tender consideration from my confreres and family soothed my psyche from the trauma and stress of the past ordeal.

By the middle of June 1999 I felt reasonably well and fit enough to start preparing for my return to Sierra Leone. Now that the Mission at Kambia and many of our schools and clinics had been totally destroyed, there were many things to provide. Through numerous friends and sympathizers I began putting together what was needed. Eventually we would organize the shipment of two 20-foot overseas containers. However, before my departure for Sierra Leone, other business had to be taken care of.

Long before my debacle with the rebels, the bishop of the diocese of Makeni, George Biguzzi, had made various commitments for me to travel to the United States for a number of mission appeals and mission animation talks in several parishes in California. In mid July, having recuperated my strength, I was off to the United States.

During my stay in America I found time to rearrange my thoughts and recollections and write a memoir of my capture. Although many friends urged me to publish it, I decided not to for the time being. There were too many names and identities of people still in power and of others who would be in jeopardy were the story to be made public.

In early September, after completing my American engagement, I went back to Italy to finalize my return to Sierra Leone planned for the end of the month. Father Franco Manganello, the parish priest of Madina, followed me to Africa about one month later. Our superiors in Rome gave us permission to return to Africa providing that we did not try to take up residence anywhere in Sierra Leone. This was sensible enough since the Kambia Mission house was gutted and Madina's Mission was still functioning as the quarters for a rebel commander in that place. Our superiors approved our plan to rent a house in Guinea in the village of Pamelap, on the border with Sierra Leone. There we were able to obtain "lassez-passer" (transit passes) from both the Guinean authorities and the rebels' command in Kambia. With those we could freely cross the border in and out on a daily basis.

In Sierra Leone the Lomé Peace Accord was in force, creating a ceasefire between the rebel forces and the government. Each side was to hold its own position while the United Nations peacekeeping force (UNAMSIL) began supervising the triple program of Disarmament, Demobilization, and Reintegration (DDR) of all fighting forces. In this atmosphere it was relatively safe to move about among the rebels in their areas, particularly if one was willing to sympathize with their miserable human conditions and extend a helping hand whenever possible. That was exactly what we set out to do, thus earning the goodwill of the grassroots rebel fighters and the protection of their leaders.

For a good eight months Father Franco and I traveled to our mission posts in Sierra Leone every day. With the help of our Christian communities, we began to reconstruct and repair the war's devastation. All was going so well that eventually we went to Conakry and bought all the basic furniture and office equipment necessary for the two mission houses of Kambia and Madina to function. We could do this thanks to money from our friends in Italy and the United States and our superiors' blessing. We stored all items in the rented house at Pamelap until it was bursting at the seams. In fact, we were in the process of requesting permission from our superiors to move to our respective mission centers and set up residence in Sierra Leone, when suddenly everything changed.

At the beginning of May 2000, for reasons difficult to fathom even to this day, the rebels pulled a fast one on the United Nations peacekeeping force. They kidnapped several contingents of the Blue Berets (the nickname of the UN Forces), a total of about 500 soldiers, and held them as hostages. That naturally ended the ceasefire, and a new state of war ensued. That also effectively ended our free movements to and from Sierra Leone. We had to confine ourselves to Guinea, hoping and waiting for a new cease-fire. We then began to devote more of our time to alleviating the misery of the many Sierra Leonean refugees who were living in the village of Pamelap and surrounding areas. It was a four-month period of works of mercy and prayer while we followed the developments across the border with great anxiety and expectation. During this period nothing else happened worthy of note for this writing, except, perhaps, the car accident and injury that I sustained.

Early on the morning of July 4, 2000, I was driving our double-cabin Toyota pickup down the paved road from Pamelap to Conakry with five passengers. While negotiating a bad curve, I lost control of the truck, and we landed in a field against the bank of a small dry brook. While the accident was not serious in terms of damage to the car—a mere small dent on the front fender—I sustained a compression fracture and resultant wedging of the L1 vertebral body.

At first it didn't seem like a major injury. I'd exited the car on my own and was able to stand and walk around while some volunteer bystanders, together with the five passengers who sustained no injury whatever, struggled to pull and push the pickup back on the road. However, it soon became obvious that I needed immediate hospitalization, for suddenly a sharp pain in my lower back almost crippled me. Fortunately on the road to Conakry there was the recently built Centre Medical Internationale run by an international staff of doctors, some of them American, which had excellent medical facilities and equipment including a CT scanner. That hospital was considered the best medical facility in Guinea. Among the five passengers traveling with me there was a driver who took control of the pickup and drove us to the hospital in little more than one hour. There a young Romanian orthopedic surgeon attended to me. After a CT scan, this doctor immobilized me in a plaster of paris body cast and later, when it became available, he fitted me with an orthopedic supportive vest that was rushed over to me by my good friend Dr. Carter Multz in San Jose, Calif.

The Romanian doctor informed me that I was very lucky to have escaped serious and permanent injury. His prognosis was that after 40 to 50 days in the cast (later, vest), I could slowly resume normal activities, but shouldn't expect a complete recovery for a full year. I first removed the orthopedic vest Aug. 22. By then I could slowly move around and climb stairs.

I felt that I had to narrate this incident since my health

condition became a critical factor in the following events. Unexpectedly, while tensions were still high among the RUF, the government of Sierra Leone, and UNAMSIL, the rebels attacked Guinea. The immediate reasons for this attack still remain obscure. The village of Pamelap was overrun, destroyed, and burned. Father Franco and I were captured. This marked the beginning of our ordeal, the second one for me.

CHAPTER EIGHT

Night Attack in Pamelap
and the Second Capture

Sept. 5, 2000, 4:15 a.m. I was awakened by the muffled sound of a big, but faraway explosion. This was immediately followed by the deafening crackle of automatic fire, thundering just next to our windows. I bounded out of bed with a spasm of pain in my back, grumbling, "Oh, not again!" I switched on my bedside battery-operated lamp. I dressed and began to round up a few essentials: the satellite phone, my documents, passport, laissez-passer, a few clothing items, toiletries, my Breviary, hunting knife, and a flashlight. I stuffed all the Mission's money—wads of Italian, Guinean, Sierra Leonean and U.S. currencies—into the pockets of the clothes I wore, putting each in a different pocket so as to minimize losing it all in the case of a hurried personal frisk.

Outside the firing was very close to the house and interspersed with reports of artillery from perhaps a quarter of a mile down the road toward the border of Sierra Leone. Giuseppe Giacomello, a volunteer attached to our Mission, knocked at my door and entered. He was living in Kambia before the big attack in February and now lived in our house with Father Franco and me. Like us he was waiting to return to the vocational school he had built and was running in Kambia and which was now obliterated. Nervous, Giuseppe asked to open the safe to retrieve his money. I motioned him to go ahead.

We both left my room to meet Father Franco. It was too noisy to ask questions, but we all wondered who was doing the shooting. Our house, situated in the center of the village of Pamelap, was only 400 yards from the military barracks, which housed some 100 Guinean regular army soldiers posted there to watch the borders. Our first assumption was that most of the shooting was from the soldiers fending off a rebel attack. The roar of the explosions was so deafening that we could hardly communicate by words. What to do? Nothing for the moment.

The shooting was coming from all directions. In fact, we couldn't even tell which was from the rebels and which was from the soldiers. It was still pitch dark outside. From the veranda door, which we had cautiously opened and left ajar (something we could safely do since our house was hidden from view by a bamboo fence), we could see and hear tracer bullets streaking and hissing in the sky. Flashes of exploding RPGs intermittently lit up housetops and trees all around. It had all the appearance of a big fireworks display, minus the thrill and plus a sense of dread. Again, there was nothing we could do!

We sat, paced, and peeked out of the veranda door while the shooting continued. At around 6 a.m., we heard the screeching and rumbling sound of war tank tracks. Days before, two large Guinean tanks had been parked by the border next to the barracks. The question now was whether the tanks were going into action or withdrawing. It was still quite dark, so we couldn't make out what was going on. We would later learn that the tanks were actually withdrawing, fleeing from the battle.

When daylight finally began to filter through, I suggested that we take flight. Giuseppe agreed wholeheartedly with his eyes rather than with words, but Father Franco, sounding reassuring, indicated that we didn't need to worry as the Guinean soldiers were the ones doing most of the shooting and were obviously holding the rebels at bay. He added, "I am going to offer Mass." It was, in fact, already 7 a.m., the regular time for the Mass we offered every day in a room of our house turned into a chapel. "Well," I said, "I'm really not in the mood to celebrate Mass but I will join with you in prayer." So, amidst the thundering chaos of a pitched battle, Father Franco celebrated Mass while I assisted.

Mass was over by 7:30. Outside the air was filled with smoke. The acrid smell of gunpowder surrounded us. On the west side of the house, a river of people flowed past, going to the north of the village. The shooting was unabated, and we still couldn't make out either soldiers or rebels. By now we all agreed, even Father Franco, that we should join the people running. We grabbed our bags and out we went into a drizzle. It was the middle of the wet season.

Giuseppe had sneaked out just minutes before the two of us, placing him some 300 or 400 yards ahead of us, thus barely escaping the trap we would fall into. A mix of men, women, and children stampeded past us and sucked us into its northward flow. There was no crying or lamenting; all were silent, frightened, and overwhelmed by the blitz.

Suddenly, just 100 yards from the house, two young warriors jumped out of nowhere, shooting their AK-47s into the ground right between and around our feet shouting, "Stop! Stop!" The two of us stopped in our tracks while the rest of the people scattered in all directions, screaming and yelling. Of course we, two white men, drew the whole attention of the young rebels. They approached closer and shot again into the ground around us, between our feet, raising bursts of dirt up to our eyes and shouting, "Stay where you are!" Father Franco shouted back, "Stop shooting! Take us to Brima Varney!" This was the commander of the brigade of RUF rebels occupying Kambia, who, we supposed, were responsible for this attack. Surprised, one of the boy-soldiers asked, "Do you know him?" Father Franco replied, "Of course, we know him. He is our friend."

"OK," the young man yelled back. His eyes were red and his gun at the ready. "OK, let's go to him, but first drop your bags and pull all the money from your pockets." With one hand on the leveled gun, one of the rebels snatched the two bags, one at a time and dragged them toward himself, while the other grabbed the money as we drew it from our pockets. They did not frisk us, so after pulling a bundle of currency starting with the Leones and then, at their insistent prompting, producing, and surrendering Guineans Francs, then Italian Lira, I motioned that that was all I had. I guess the Italian Lira impressed them as good foreign currency. Little did they know that Italian Lira were less valuable than even their Leones and the Guinean Francs. They did not insist for more and thus I was able to withhold the $900 American dollars that I had stuffed in one side pocket.

Following the rebels' directives, we marched in front of them along the main street of the village toward the Guineans' military barracks. Dead bodies were strewn all around, mostly in Guinean uniform. By now the shooting had become less intense. The more we advanced, the more rebels we met: mostly young, red-eyed, perhaps from drugs or alcohol, wearing red scarves on their neck or head. Many were unshod and coarsely dressed; some wore flamboyant bandoliers across their chests and all were armed to the teeth with both heavy and light automatic weapons, hand grenades, RPGs and the like.

After 10 minutes of walking we rounded a bend in the road and came face to face with the "high command" of the rebels' 2nd Brigade headquartered in Kambia: Brig. Gen. Brima Varney, Colonels Sandy, Joe, Ezekiel, and others. They were sitting under a big oak tree, surrounded by their orderlies. It seemed to me that upon seeing us they felt embarrassed. Obviously they were not expecting to see us in Pamelap, even though they should have known that we were living there. Perhaps they thought that we had been alerted and had left before the attack.

We knew them well, of course. These were the very people

we had repeatedly met with and helped before in Kambia or Madina. These were the people who had issued us a laissez-passer to their territories, who had proclaimed that they wanted peace and no more war; and who even had asked us to convey their wishes to the Guinean, Sierra Leonean, and UN authorities. Now here they were, directing a fierce attack on a neutral country.

Their presence heartened us at first, particularly because we could see their embarrassment. But after the handshakes and the first expressions of regret for our capture, we understood that we had fallen into a trap; and in the trap we had to remain. Colonel Joe (a Catholic), explained that they were sorry that we had been captured, as they had not foreseen this situation. At any rate we must now have patience and stay with them, since, for reasons of war, they could neither let us go, nor return to us our belongings and money. (We learned later the reasons for our detention, which indeed had to do with war and the secrecy of the rebels' movements regarding the international community.) But, they added, we could rest assured that no harm would come to us and that they, the rebels, would take good care of us as long as we followed their instructions.

Thereupon Colonel Joe, who was the commander of their military police, called another officer of lower rank, Major Jalloh, and gave him strict orders to take good care of us. When it was both possible and safe, he was to take us to the guard post on the other side of the Great Scarcies river, some five miles before entering Kambia. With that we were led away from the scene of the battle. Fighting was still going on all around us, and the risk of injury from aimed or stray bullets and grenade explosions was very real.

The drizzle of the early morning was now turning into light rain and, on the way to our new destination, we stopped and took cover in one of the buildings of the so-called "New Customs." the Sierra Leone facility for cross-border transactions. This was empty now, of course, and was half a mile away from the thick of the fire, which was now of a different nature.

Guinean reinforcements were beginning to respond to the rebels' attack with heavy mortar rounds and heavy machine guns. Shells began to fall all around us and the danger of being hit became quite pressing. As we sat on the steps of the customs house, sheltered from the rain, we could see a constant flow of rebel troops passing by, to and from Kambia and Pamelap. All sorts of stolen vehicles were being used and soon I spotted our own two Toyota pickups ferrying looted goods from Pamelap. Not having the ignition keys to start the engines, the rebels had broken into the vehicles, smashed their steering wheel locks, and cross-wired them.

CHAPTER NINE

First Day in the Hands
of the Rebels in Pamelap

Briefed by Father Franco of my traffic accident, and in consideration of my injury, Colonel Joe dispatched a fighter to order us to wait for a vehicle that would take us to the guard post in Kambia on the other side of the Kolenten River. It was nine in the morning. Our waiting place had become a stopover for dozens of rebels returning on foot from Pamelap a mile away, loaded with all sorts of looted property. They would stash their war booty, as they called it, in several rooms of the customs house, leaving it in the care of the rebels' orderlies. Then off they'd go for more looting and killing. Many of the guerrillas were children, and they too had their loot: candies, lollipops, cigarettes, rubber balls, toys, radios, tapes and bicycles. Most of the rebels, including the children, were drinking stolen beer and/or liquor. Especially common was the so-called "Gin pack," a plastic blister pack containing 12 four-ounce blisters of cheap gin. The rebels had thousands of these packets stolen from various bars or shops. They laughed and celebrated, reveling in the success of their attack, even though it was still under way.

From time to time rebels would arrive in droves: pushing, pulling and taunting the prisoners. In one instance a group of young rebels approached the customs house dragging and shoving a prisoner. Father Franco recognized one of the rebels whom they called Hamid Pull-eye, who was known to specialize in gouging out eyes with his bare hands.

The middle-aged prisoner, we later learned, was a Guinean customs officer. He had been captured barely an hour before. His face was dripping blood onto his shirt from a cutlass (a West Africa machete) gash across his scalp. The rebels, obviously high, were creating a din. As they approached the steps where we were sitting, they forced their victim to sit on a nearby tree stump while they shouted and jeered.

While one grabbed the poor man by his hair, tilting his face upward, others immobilized him. Then the infamous gouger, Hamid Pull-eye, resting his left hand on the victim's right shoulder, extended his right index finger, which was topped with a long, sharp nail, intending to penetrate the eye socket and gouge out the eyeball. The poor wretch, realizing what was about to happen, began screaming at the top of his lungs amidst the laughter and roaring of the horde around him. At this point both Franco and I jumped up and threw our weight against the attackers, breaking the vicious lock. I shouted, "Stop this! What are you doing? Stop it!"

For a split second I thought we were finished, since we were surrounded by drunk and drugged men, all armed to the teeth. But obviously our turn had not yet come. At first all of the rabble were stunned by our sudden intervention. Then there was a cacophony of shouting: "He is an enemy! He is a soldier and he was out to kill us!" I retorted, "He is not a soldier. Don't you see the way he's dressed? I know the man, and he is not a soldier." "He is not?" the gouger asked. "I assure you, he is not!" I replied.

Then Major Jalloh, the officer charged with our safety, ordered, "Leave him alone." I prompted, "Let him sit here by us and we will take full responsibility for him." So they let him sit on the step next to us, and for the time being he was delivered from their hands.

Given the top commanders' orders not to harm us, we knew that no one in his right mind would want to harass us. Besides the direct protection of Major Jalloh at our side, we were well recognized by many of them as the "Fathers" who had helped them so many times when they were in need. Even their big leaders had shaken our hands with respect.

All this, of course, was reassuring only to a point. What if we came face to face with some young rebels who didn't know us or were under the influence of drugs and alcohol? There were so many of them milling around! Their languages and accents clearly indicated that many had come from distant parts. Later we learned that at least a thousand men and boys from three different brigades had carried out the attack on Pamelap.

At one point a youngster came forward, his AK-47 almost bigger than he, at the ready. Wobbling on his feet, his eyes bloodshot, with a mocking sneer he ordered Father Franco, "You, white man, open your mouth." With that he stuck the muzzle of his rifle between Father's lips, pushing to pry his jaws open. Eventually, with a snort, he managed to shove the gun right into the priest's mouth. Before I could say a word, Major Jalloh, who had turned aside to relieve himself, came from behind and with a swipe of his hand struck the warrior on his neck at the base of his head knocking him flat, his gun falling beside him.

"You stupid jerk, what do you think you're doing?" he shouted at the young rebel, kicking him while he still lay on the ground. "I would have you shot!"

"I beg you, I beg, I'm sorry, sir," the boy whimpered and, pulling himself up, he scuttled away.

Jalloh then apologized to Father, remarking that obviously the boy did not know us. Precisely! How many of these encounters were we to have in the days or nights ahead, particularly when our "friends" were nowhere near to protect us?

A group of the fighters came around telling us that they were in fact RUF, which they could hardly deny since we recognized so many of them. They said, "We are not here on behalf of the movement, but only to help the Guinean rebels start their own revolution against the dictator Lansana Conteh (the current president of the Republic of Guinea). We really are mercenaries of our Guinean brothers."

Others in the group were claiming that they were rebels from Burkina Faso or from Liberia. Still others declared themselves members of the RFDG, Rassemblement des Forces

Démocratiques de Guinée. However, the heavy accent of these last ones gave them away; they could not possibly be French-speaking Guineans. We supposed they were trying to impress upon us that whatever was happening was not an official operation of the RUF.

By 10:30 the small weapons shooting had become less intense, but the heavy artillery of the Guineans had become more insistent. Shells were dropping all around us with a shattering noise. Although the rain was now a heavy downpour, the movement of the rebel troops and vehicles was incessant. Finally a Mercedes Benz came by with Colonel Joe. We and a number of rebels piled in, and off we went. This car, like all those commandeered by the fighters, had a bashed-in dashboard, wires hanging, and a shattered rear window through which the rebels gained entry into the car.

After three miles we ran out of gas, and all got out to push except me, who was expressly excused by Colonel Joe in view of my back injury. Suddenly a jeep full of rebels appeared coming from the opposite direction. The colonel stopped it and commandeered it to take us to the guard post, only two miles ahead.

We reached our first prison station. It was very near to the town of Kambia, just 200 yards from the Kolenten River. It was a spacious house seized by the rebels from its rightful owner, just like all of the houses still remaining standing in Kambia. Colonel Joe assigned us to a two-room suite, which had a handwritten label at the entrance reading "Officers' Mess." In one room there were five bare, large wicker armchairs and a small wicker center table. The other room had a big straw mattress on the floor, which could accommodate up to three persons. The Guinean immigration officer was left with us under our protection for four more days.

Colonel Joe introduced us to the guard-post commander, Capt. John, and insisted that we were to be taken care of as comfortably as possible under the circumstances. There must have been at least 20 other rebels in residence in the house occupying several rooms. In a separate large room they kept several other prisoners. Most were Guineans, but RUF rebel dissenters were detained as well. They were all lying on the bare cement floor and were locked in day and night. We, however, could move about the house and the immediate surroundings, although we noticed that we were constantly under surveillance by armed men. Before leaving, Colonel Joe told us that he would use all possible means to have us released soon, maybe in a few days. We were now six miles from the battlefront. We could still hear shooting and cannon shells falling around us from time to time, but it was nothing like the racket and deafening explosions of the battlefield.

The guardhouse stood right alongside the main highway connecting Kambia and Pamelap, so we could witness the endless and incessant traffic of cars and trucks. For the nine days we stayed there the rebels transported looted property day and night.

The first night, in spite of my tiredness, I couldn't sleep. I would lie down on the straw mattress and then get up, sit in one of the bare wicker chairs, then try the straw mattress again. The rain was incessant; thank God, for it provided us with potable water.

In the darkness, still under the threat of falling shells and rockets that exploded here and there within a radius of 300 yards and with the background crackling of faraway automatic weapons, I began to pray the Rosary. I would do this intermittently throughout our ordeal. At the beginning of every decade I inserted an additional invocation of my own: *"In manus tuas, Domine, commendo spiritum meum."* (Into your hands, Lord, I commend my spirit.)

The thought occurred to me that by this second, successive and total loss of everything material I had gathered to re-establish our Mission—thousands of dollars worth of goods—perhaps God was telling me that I was "barking up the wrong tree." Or was it perhaps that I had not been found worthy of shepherding his flock? Under stress and apprehension, all kinds of thoughts can come to one's mind. And in the darkness (both physical and psychological) several times I caught myself crying. May God forgive me. I couldn't help it.

CHAPTER TEN

Eight Days of Confinement at the Guardhouse

Sitting on the veranda of that big house, always flanked by two armed young rebels, I stared straight ahead absentmindedly. In the twilight I could see the traffic of trucks, cars and motorcycles moving slowly on the highway just 50 yards from the house. It was a constant movement of troops and of looted material to and from Pamelap. Shooting was still going on and cannon balls still flying.

Soon we began to receive our first visitors. Rebels! A truck slowed down and swung inside the front yard of the guardhouse. A child-soldier, no more than 12 years old, jumped down and ran to us shouting, "Father Franco, Father Franco!" He dropped his rifle and jumped up to hug Father Franco. Father recognized him. It was Joseph, a member of the children's choir of his Mission church at Madina. Father Franco introduced us, and Joseph shook my hand vigorously. He was anxious to know how we were being treated. He declared that he had been promoted to first aide de camp to Colonel Joe and was now an important person! He picked up the big AK-47 and held it in his hand with obvious pride. It was an incredible scene; much older rebels looked at the child with some amusement and yet with deference.

Joseph was full of attention for us, inquiring where we had put up for the night, if we had food, if anyone had harassed us, and so on. We thanked him for his concern and assured him that— given the circumstances—everything was OK. He added to Father Franco, "I'm sorry, Father, for what has happened to you. But don't worry. You and your friend will be out of here in no time. You will see! I will come back soon." He turned and headed toward the waiting truck. Then he suddenly stopped, turned around and coming back to us, he pulled a wad of money from his pocket. He counted out ten thousand Leones (about $7.00 in U.S. currency). Pressing the notes into Father's hand, he said, "Here, have something from me!" and scurried away. Father Franco and I were speechless.

People started coming in droves from the direction of Pamelap. They were Sierra Leonean refugees who had taken shelter in Pamelap, during the years of rebel activity in Sierra Leone. Now they were caught between two fires: the invading RUF rebels on one side and the counterattacking Guinean army on the other. They were running back from Guinea into their own country, and the rebels were apparently letting them through. They made a sorry sight—men, women, and children toting or dragging whatever little they were able to salvage. Many stopped by the guardhouse for a short rest, some asking for water to drink and others buying fruit or cake from peddlers from Kambia.

Many recognized us and we them. In seeing us as prisoners

of the rebels they sympathized with our plight and offered encouragement, which, coming from people under such a deprivation and stress of their own moved us almost to tears. We heartily reciprocated their sentiments. We consoled each other and found some relief in our common misfortune. The rebel guards were rather accommodating to the twice-routed refugees and generally did not harass them. There were heartbreaking exceptions, however, as when a young rebel with flimsy excuses would "confiscate" goods from the miserable load of the fleeing people.

We used these encounters to find out about people close to us: colleagues, neighbors, teachers, catechists, and others of whom we had lost sight. Also, since some of the fleeing refugees were heading to the capital city, Freetown, I surreptitiously scribbled a note directed to our confreres there. I informed them of our capture and advised them to disconnect from the overseas office our satellite phone that had fallen into rebel hands together with our bags.

At 5 p.m. on that first day, Capt. John called us over to the small shack that served as his residence to listen to the BBC News broadcast "Focus on Africa." The reception was very clear. The first item was the announcement of the attack on Pamelap. The announcer broadcast: "Reportedly the Sierra Leone RUF invaded Guinea again, this time at the border with the village of Pamelap, purportedly in support of their counterpart Guinean rebels." After the news, an analysis and comments on the events of the day routinely followed. That day there was an interview with Gibril Massaquoi, the official spokesman of the RUF at their Makeni headquarters. The BBC commentator, Robin White I believe, said on a satellite phone line to Gibril Massaquoi, "Regarding your attack at Pamelap, the bishop of Makeni, George Biguzzi, has reported that two of his missionaries have been captured by your men. Where are the missionaries now?"

Gibril Massaquoi replied (in these words or similar): "Missionaries?! What missionaries? We do not capture missionaries anywhere. We are not holding any missionaries! Pamelap? What Pamelap? We have nothing to do with Pamelap. We have nothing to do with Guinea. We are Sierra Leoneans. Our interest is right here in our country." Every one of the rebel bystanders laughed loudly at Massaquoi's response. Capt. John asked me, "What do you say about that, Father Victor?"

More loud laughter. I answered, "Well, either Mr. Massaquoi has not been informed or he is a big liar." The laughter turned into roars. Lying through their teeth has always been second nature for the RUF. One could never believe or be sure of anything they said. My long experience with the rebels was that lying was an integral part of their behavior, even for the best intentioned of them. Their general principle was that the end justifies the means. Even though good intentions, if often misguided, were quite common with the RUF, subsequent developments would create new situations that in their mind justified the complete reneging on the good intentions they had previously sworn by. Consequently their word had no value whatsoever. Even though I had learned all this during my first capture and detention, it took further bitter experience for it to sink in.

Day after day we remained confined to the guardhouse. We ate the rebels' food once a day and drank rainwater—thank God for that—but we could not wash, change clothes or shave. Even during the rain season in Sierra Leone it is always stiflingly hot and our clothes became uncomfortable and smelly. At first I thought the young rebels around were emitting bad odors, but then I suddenly realized it was me smelling, not so much them. Of course, the commotion all around us didn't allow for much brooding over this.

One time when Colonel Joe came by, we complained that up to that day we had not been able to wash or change clothes. He then gave us permission to go to a nearby brook, a branch of the Kolenten River, to wash – accompanied by armed escort. Additionally he ordered a bundle of assorted clothes and two bars of scented soap to be given to us. We were thankful for them, even though we felt guilty as we well realized that all those clothes and soap were stolen goods, part of the looting at Pamelap.

Our immediate concern was to stay clear of stray bullets and shells. However our underlying apprehension was about what would happen to us when the rebels experienced reversal and had to run. The assurances of Colonel Joe and his colleagues did nothing to allay our fears because we had begun to lose hope in their promises. We understood perfectly well the predicament of our local rebels: having radioed our capture to their authorities at headquarters in Makeni, their hands were now tied as to releasing us. They were totally dependent upon orders from above. We had become two very inconvenient witnesses of what really had happened in Pamelap—and this at a critical time, when the RUF was trying to convince the international community that the movement had nothing to do with the attack on Guinea. This was the "reasons of war" that the rebels had referred to at our capture to explain why they couldn't release us immediately.

To sweeten the pill of their refusal to let us go, Brig. Gen. Brima Varney and Colonels Joe, Ezekiel, and Matthew suggested that we could be moved from Kambia, to our own mission house in Madina. We wholeheartedly approved this proposal, of course. It was now eight days and nights that we had been holed up in the guardhouse, by the Kolenten River.

CHAPTER ELEVEN

Destination: Madina, Tonko Limba

In the late afternoon of Sept. 9, Colonel Joe announced, "I have obtained permission from the brigade commander to transfer the two of you to Madina. Stand ready to leave in an hour's time." Madina was Father Franco's Mission center, 25 miles north of Kambia. We both were happy with this decision. It was infinitely better to be confined in one's own house rather than in a guard post, which was more like a jail with all sorts of people coming and going. Besides, our release (that we still naively hoped our rebel "friends" would soon obtain) would be more likely to occur at Madina rather than at Kambia, since the latter was now the war front.

Since we had nothing to prepare, we were ready in no time. The colonel's Peugeot sedan, one of the commandeered vehicles from Pamelap, picked us up along with four bodyguards armed with AK 47 rifles and RPGs. They drove first to Kambia's Checkpoint, only half a mile away, in order to stop at the colonel's house to pick up drugs for me to fight off a malaria attack that I felt was coming on. After obtaining the medication, we proceeded through downtown Kambia toward Madina.

Everywhere we passed we saw destruction, desolation and

emptiness. On the left the police barracks had been reduced to a row of battered and empty shells, riddled with bullet holes. To our right, opposite the barracks, stood one of our two elementary schools in Kambia town, the St. Augustine Police Barracks Primary School. The masonry structure built only four years earlier, made to serve 500 children, was now in shambles. The walls were still standing but they were pocked with bullets and grenade holes. The roof was completely gone. Only the new wooden frame of the roof, that I built recently during the months I traveled back and forth from Pamelap, was visible. The frame looked like a while skeleton resting on burned walls.

Down the road, we passed through the Kambia District Prisons compound. On the left were the prison's officers' quarters, now a big heap of rubble; and on the right was the prison itself. All the corrugated zinc of the roof was gone, and the building was left in crumbled ruins without a single wall standing. As we continued on, approaching the center of town, we arrived at a rebel checkpoint. A few child soldiers in tattered clothes slouched down under a nearby grass roof. As the car approached, at first nobody moved. But as soon as they recognized the colonel in the front seat, they all jumped and rushed to raise the barrier pole. We passed.

On the right side of the road stood the Kambia District Council Center, one of the few buildings in Kambia still substantially intact. It was a two-story, cement block structure, which now functioned as the second brigade of the RUF headquarters. Next to it was the Kambia District Council (DC) Government Primary School built to accommodate more than 1,000 children. It was in ruins, with the roof's corrugated zinc gone, torn off and stolen. On the left, opposite the school, was the newly roofed "Under Five" Clinic, now deserted. The Doctors Without Borders (MSF or Medicins Sans Frontieres) of Holland had rebuilt this clinic and had resumed its operation just before the kidnapping of the 500 UNAMSIL soldiers. Like us in rebuilding our two Mission posts, the MSF had worked out of a temporary headquarters in Pamelap. Only they were luckier (or more foresighted) than us in that their Dutch director had ordered them out of Pamelap about a month before the attack.

We were now at the center of Kambia town. Everywhere we looked, it was the same depressing scene. What used to be a lively, teeming, and humming place had become a bleak, uninhabited desert. I had an eerie feeling through all of this! At a fork in the dirt road we took Hospital Street, toward Madina, away from our Mission house and church.

It was on this street that the only general hospital in the whole District was located. It was a 153-bed facility, with two operating theaters, an emergency room, labs, a pharmacy and a number of specialized clinics attached to it, plus an entire block of nurses' quarters. Now only the charred walls stood. The roof was gone, the zinc pans stolen, the wood frame burned down and all equipment and furnishings destroyed, looted or burned.

Taking Kukuna Road, which led through the last part of

Kambia town and on toward Madina, we passed between the main St. Augustine Primary School on the right, a facility for 900 children, and the coeducational Kolenten Secondary School: a complex of several concrete buildings with classrooms, labs, and administrative offices for a high school of 500 students. Both were schools of the Catholic Mission and both were now completely gutted. Only the new wood frames of the roofs, which I had recently erected, still remained.

The very day the peace process collapsed with the kidnapping of the UNAMSIL soldiers, I had been able by satellite phone to suspend delivery from Freetown of 10,000 square feet of zinc roofing sheets. I had them shipped from Italy by ocean freight at the cost of thousands of U.S. dollars. They were to cover the 15 roofs of all our facilities in Kambia town. The truck had been stopped in time. Thus we were able to save the zinc for later use.

Obstructed by a cluster of trees, the Xaverian Sisters' house and the Rehabilitation Center for Poliomyelitic Children were not visible from the Kukuna Road, but I knew that they too were completely burned and destroyed.

Leaving Kambia behind, we proceeded very slowly on the treacherous, narrow, and winding dirt road through thick bush, from village to village, toward Madina. By now darkness had descended and we were not able to contemplate the devastation reported by our people. Almost every village along the way had had a school or a clinic or a church. Now, who knew how many were still standing? Certainly all had been looted. People had scattered. The remaining few, forced to cooperate with the rebels, were aware that in the future the government forces would accuse them of collaborating with the enemy. They would be victims of both sides.

The road was awful, looking at times like a river whose banks were formed by the lines of trees and surrounding bushes. We finally arrived in front of the dilapidated Mission house of Madina late that night. The colonel let us off there with a couple of his bodyguards. We could take possession of the empty building but were under strict orders to confine ourselves there. Three Mission boys materialized from nowhere. Father Franco knew them well, as they had been entrusted with the keys of the front door when he had left in a hurry, following the collapse of the ceasefire. Now the boys who were also physically in bad shape, welcomed us and let us in. We entered our house as prisoners. Reciprocal commiseration and sympathy followed.

The place was hot, humid and dark. It stunk of an unidentifiable and indescribable smell. We both were too tired to indulge in long conversation or even to think of food. We drank some water from the Mission well, and finding our way by candlelight, located some camp beds in two rooms. There we lay down, resting our bones and waiting for the light of the new day to shed the darkness and let us appraise the situation.

CHAPTER TWELVE

Seventy-Nine Days Under House Arrest in Madina

The Setting and the First Day

As the first light of dawn began filtering through the windows, I woke up, dazed and wondering where I was. Oh, yes. And that's the stench I remember smelling in the darkness the night before. Now I could see. The walls of the room were spattered with something red. Paint? I reached out with one hand to the nearest blotch. It was dry, caked. Could it be blood? That must be the reason for the stench. At this point Father Franco appeared in the doorway. "Yes," he said, "it's blood. God only knows what they have been doing in this house during their occupancy. I removed most of the filth, but I couldn't clean the whole house."

He was referring to the time before present hostilities resumed, when he was coming from Pamelap every day to repair and restore the house—installing windows and doors, patching holes in the walls, and scraping up the encrusted filth that had accumulated everywhere during the months of the first rebel occupation of the premises.

The muffled sound of mortar explosions came from far away. Madina was about eight miles from the Sierra Leone-

Guinean border, and the Guinean army was shelling rebel positions. Grenades occasionally fell around and within the village but their impact was not as threatening as it had been at the Kolenten Bridge in Kambia.

Father Franco encouraged me to follow him through the house, and he showed me the work he had been doing up to the time we had stopped coming to Sierra Leone and holed up in Pamelap. The Mission boys also came round, happy to see us: Moses, Sulaiman, Phillip, Alhaji, and others. Eager to assist, they fetched water for drinking and washing.

I should point out that the condition of the Mission compound upon this, our second return as prisoners under house arrest, was very different from the condition of Father Franco's first return after the 11 months of rebel occupation of the house. At that time, in October 1999, the house was standing, but everything inside was gone, including the furniture, toilets, sinks, light fixtures, and even electrical cables. They'd been ripped from the wall and the ceiling: switches, plugs, everything. Even the windows and doorframes were gone, and some walls were bashed in to access closets or supposed hideaways. In the eight months since our return from Italy, Father Franco had repaired much of the damage.

Now the boys produced pails, buckets, and other implements, that they, who were residing in the Mission, had cleverly hidden immediately following the kidnapping of the UN troops.

While we were inspecting the various rooms, Captain Kelvin, a young rebel in charge of security and a longtime friend of Father Franco's even before the revolution, came to us. He wore military fatigues and was accompanied by three other rebels not dressed as well as he, but all armed to the hilt.

Captain Kelvin appeared exuberant and pleasant. After shaking hands, he inquired if we had had a good night's sleep and if we found the house congenial. With a laugh Father Franco remarked, "It's our house, and even though it's missing most of its furniture, it suits us perfectly." Actually, after the nine nights of sleeping on the floor of a prison, these accommodations, if not exactly luxurious, were definitely much better. We thanked the captain and assured him that we were fine and satisfied with the new arrangement.

Then the captain assumed a somber, somewhat stern expression. "Fathers, make yourselves at home. But understand that you must not leave the compound at any time. Orders from Colonel Joe. He will soon come himself to see you. In the meantime we will be around." With that, in sharp contrast to his previous exuberance, he and his escorts turned around and left. We understood quite well what he meant. From the windows we could see several armed young rebels strategically positioned at key points around the Mission.

We decided to go across the backyard to see the church, Our Lady of the Angels, Father Franco's "parish" church. It was a hexagonal brick structure built south of the Mission house.

The building was still intact with the exception of a few bullet holes here and there.

Madina did not suffer the total destruction that other places such as Kambia had. The results of looting and vandalism were seen everywhere. But the boys told us that there was no destruction of buildings in Madina. Although the church had been looted of most of its furnishings, the foot pedal harmonium (an old-fashioned organ) was still there and working. Father Franco, musician that he was, immediately tested the instrument; and a joyful stream of harmonic strains filled the air, drawing several children to the windows of the church. Gesticulating excitedly, they cried out in Krio language, "Fatha Franco don come! Fatha don come!"

Here too, in the church as in the house, the Mission boys had saved and hidden much that could have been looted or spoiled: vestments, sacred vessels, candlesticks, large and small hosts with a little wine for the Eucharist, and so forth. They pulled out all these things from above the ceiling of their sleeping quarters. They even produced a set of plastic arm chairs, some basic kitchen appliances and, praise God, an Italian espresso coffeemaker, with a small bag of ground coffee, still air-sealed! Father Franco had trained them well.

As we returned to the house, we began to plan our living space. Father Franco would take his old office near the main entrance, and the adjacent bedroom where, miraculously, the bed and mattresses remained although everything else was gone.

I set up my quarters in the guest bedroom. In it there was a small iron bed with a new mattress! Connected to the room was a full bath that was partially damaged. The basin of the shower stall had been pried up with a crowbar; I suppose to find out if anything might be hidden underneath the stall, such as diamonds, money or weapons. The plumbing system wasn't working, as pipes were dangling all over the place. Because there were no tables or chairs in my new bedroom, I made my desk out of the platform of a heavy combined electric sawing and plane machine that occupied the central floor of the adjacent carpentry workshop situated at the very end of the house. By lowering the heavy sawing blade of the machine until it disappeared underneath the level of the plane's blades, I created a steel platform where I could lay books and write. Never in my whole life did I have a desk as solid and massive as that! In effect, I was settled at the very back of the long house and Father Franco at the very front, with the rooms of the clinic between us.

Around midday Colonel Joe arrived with a number of his orderlies. A big smile on his face, he asked how we were doing and if we liked the new setup. We said we did and thanked him, for we knew it was he who had convinced those in the high command to allow our transfer from the prison in Kambia. Father Franco immediately asked why we were to be confined to the mission compound. Colonel Joe said, "If you promise me that you will not attempt anything foolish, I will allow you to walk around town." We promised, and we were free to stroll around Madina.

Then the colonel motioned to a couple of his orderlies to bring in a supply of food: a 100-pound bag of rice, two gallons of palm oil, two packets of Magi cubes, assorted cans of fish, meat, salads and fruit. Everything, we were afraid, had been looted from stores in Pamelap. Although we suspected that much, it was all we had to eat. So we thanked him, just as we had done when he'd had the clothes sent over for us at the prison in Kambia. Given the circumstances, what else could we have done?

By late afternoon the news had spread that Father Franco and another Father were in the Mission. Villagers from Madina and surrounding villages began flocking to the house to greet us and wish us well. With the civilians were also many rebels, who were posted in and around Madina and who had known us for a long time. Many of them knew Father Franco even before they joined the rebels. They all came to see the Fathers, to greet us, sympathize with us and to bring various gifts, mostly foodstuffs, as tokens of support. It was a great show of solidarity, quite moving and encouraging. None of this deterred the attentive vigilance of the guards posted in strategic locations around the Mission, watching our every move. This vigilance was to decrease with the passage of days and nights. In fact, after a couple of weeks, nobody from the rebels' security force seemed to pay much attention to us, with the exception, of course, of the many rebels, some of higher rank, who daily made friendly visits to talk with us and assure us that soon we would be released. This empty promise began to sound almost like a derisive joke.

As evening drew on, visitors began to diminish. But another crowd began to assemble by the church. These were the faithful parishioners coming for evening prayer. Alhaji, one of the Mission boys, climbed up the small bell tower and rang the bell for devotions. The Mission boys produced a couple of kerosene lanterns that they had retrieved from the hiding place. We proceeded to the church, while Father Franco, seated at the harmonium, filled the church and surrounding area with beautiful music. The larger kerosene lamp was placed on the altar, the smaller one at the entrance of the church. More people flowed in.

We all prayed the Holy Rosary. I had chosen to kneel in an empty pew, but soon found myself surrounded by a dozen or so little worshippers, five or six years old, who sat one next to the other. They sat clustered among themselves like a flock of birds, pressing against me on both sides with typical African coziness. That really was like praying with angels!

After the Rosary Father Franco announced that starting the next day we would offer Holy Mass every morning at 7 a.m. and would close every day with the evening Rosary. Then David, the catechist, addressed the 50 or so in the congregation. He spoke first in Krio and then in Limba, urging them to spread the word that now that the Fathers had arrived, life at the Mission would resume as "usual"—whatever that word "usual" might have meant for him or them.

Father Franco was full of life and, I would almost say, exuberant. I, on the other hand, felt rather depressed, though I tried not to show it. My mind was in Pamelap and in Kambia where my Mission lay wrecked, my people scattered and ravaged by ongoing battles. In the distance we could hear heavy artillery. After prayers most of the people disappeared into the darkness around the church.

September is in the middle of the rainy season in West Africa. Light rain had been coming down all through the day, but in late evening it began to pour. Under the zinc roof it was deafening. Still, the Mission boys, their friends, and also some rebel child soldiers, clustered around us in the small lobby of the Mission house.

We sat by the light of a kerosene lantern. Father Franco and I sat on the plastic chairs saved by the Mission boys and the others were squatting on the floor. Still others sat on local African mini stools that people oftentimes carried around with them. At first they were waiting for the rain to abate, but then they stayed on to enjoy our company. In spite of the noise of the rain, everyone was full of questions. Typically, everyone talked at the same time. Every one of them wanted to know something and, of course, so did we. For a while we were almost yelling over the crashing of the rain, but after a while the heavy downpour subsided and we could conduct a normal conversation.

It was getting late and we had to excuse ourselves to retire. Artillery explosions could still be heard coming from the Guinean border west of us. Obviously the firing was not directed toward Madina, because there was no report of falling projectiles or grenades. I took the smaller kerosene lantern and went to my room at the other end of the long building.

As I was about to remove my clothes to prepare for bed, I heard a clatter of machine gun fire not too far from the village, but still toward the Guinean border. The thought was immediate: they are coming! We were expecting the Guineans to mount a counterattack both to avenge the assault on Pamelap and to flush out the RUF rebels. The crackling sound of automatic fire was ominous to me.

I decided to walk back to Father Franco and consult with him on the new development. He said, "Yes, I hear the gunfire. They may perhaps be fighting with small groups infiltrating from the border. Who knows? However, I don't think it is anything big. Let's hope it's nothing really serious. Have courage! Good night!" I returned, mulling this over. I was tired and wanted to lie down. I wanted to sleep but could not bring myself to take off my clothes. In spite of the heat I decided to lie in bed fully dressed, ready to leap up and run if the need should arise. The new mattress was comfortable, firm yet springy, and I relished lying there; yet sleep did not come until much later in the night.

Eventually I did fall asleep, my mind fraught with foreboding.

People and Activities

I think it would be useful to give a bird's-eye view of conditions, people and things as they appeared to us during the 79 days we were in detention at Madina. Most events revolved around these six topics: life, church, people, friends, rebels and boys (both child soldiers and village boys).

Life: Our life under house arrest was a sequence of simple events hinging on survival, prayer, reading, and advising both rebels and villagers. We realized, and were thankful, that as long as things went well for the RUF, we would be left undisturbed and might even enjoy a certain degree of respect and security. However, the specter always hung over us that in case of military reverses, when retreat should become necessary for the rebels, we would be expected to flee on foot with them. In such circumstances both respect and security would become very relative or completely vanish.

The previous year such a situation of retreat and running on foot, as envisioned here, did occur. Three nuns and one priest were either shot dead or left to die on the rebels' escape trail in the mountains of the western area. At that time the RUF and the AFRC (SL army deserters) that had formed the junta were pushed out of Freetown and retreated.

This foreboding was all the more terrifying because every day and night we could hear the sustained rumbling of gunfire and explosions coming from various, relatively nearby, locations.

We witnessed the constant, at times frantic, movement of the rebels in transit between Kamaqui, Kambia, Rokupr, Port Loko, Lunsar, and Makeni. Madina was the obligatory connecting point of the main centers of the RUF stationed in the northern province of Sierra Leone.

Particularly sinister were the night movements. In pitch darkness the silence was broken alternatively by mortar explosions and automatic fire, along with trucks thundering past. These movements were mingled with the voices of hundreds of blustering young guerrillas, en route to some unknown front. Pamelap? Freetown? A new point of entry into Guinea? We couldn't tell. This supercharged atmosphere was the reality, and we had to cope with it—but it was difficult to keep calm.

Church: In this threatening context our prayer life became particularly meaningful. A great source of courage and strength were community prayers: Holy Mass, the Divine Office, the Rosary, and other devotions we conducted and organized with the villagers either in the church or in places adjacent to the Mission.

Father Franco was particularly resourceful in organizing church and devotional services. His expertise in music, as a true maestro trained in the conservatories of Italy, enabled him to set up a lively choir of men, women and children of the village. Even some of the rebels joined the choir. The old pedal organ, that had miraculously escaped destruction or even tampering, was a great means of calling people together. Father's ingenuity and courage served to create a prayerful setting in the bare church, which had been looted of most of its appointments.

Mass was at 7 a.m. and choir practice was in the afternoon. Rosary and evening prayers were at 8 p.m., at which time the sacrament of reconciliation was made available to anyone desiring to receive it. This schedule of church activities was carried out whenever there was not the interference of unexpected war events, which unfortunately occurred quite often. On Sundays the Mass was at 9 a.m. The small church was always filled to capacity, standing room only, and a number of RUF too would participate, some of rank, such as captains, majors and colonels. Thank God! Remarkably, none of the higher rank ever came forward to receive Communion. I wonder what our response would have been in such a case. We requested that all rebels who wished to attend Mass leave their weapons outside the church. They mostly complied!

Father Franco and I used to take turns presiding at Mass and delivering the sermon. Both of us used this opportunity to stress how contrary violence was to Jesus' teachings, and how necessary it was for all to forgive injustices instead of making them a pretext for more violence. Sometimes the urgings, warnings, and condemnations were quite stern and direct; I would almost say thundering. But, interestingly and to our relief, no one protested nor showed resentment.

Prayer life was not confined to church. People from the village, including the rebels, called us to their houses for special prayers over the sick, the dying and the dead. We held three Christian funerals during that time. It was usually Father Franco who responded to these calls, since he was the actual pastor of the area and knew his people well.

One evening the rebels held an ecumenical prayer service, Christians and Muslims together, for all the comrades who had fallen in a recent battle on the Guinean border. Father Franco went to the house where the event took place, along with the church choir and our drummers. When he returned, later that night, he told me how the house was filled with rebels of all ranks. In fact, there was no room to accommodate everyone, and more than half of the crowd had to squat on the ground outside, around the house. The service, conducted by torchlight, included singing, prayers and reading of the Holy Bible by the Christians and the Holy Quran by several Imams.

All this was interspersed with sporadic shooting in the immediate area and the faraway rumbling of artillery fire. The event lasted well over two hours.

We had the clear impression that the rebels were encouraging this turn of events in the parish. I remembered the explicit proposals made to me by a rebel commander during my previous detention and understood that the rebels wanted us to function as pastors, organizing church and school activities. This and other efforts, like that of keeping alive the weekly regional market called the "luma" would make a positive impression on people in town and visitors from out of town. The rebels wanted to be seen as sociable people, civic-minded and quite capable of establishing a well-organized society complete with judicial courts, police, school, market and religious activities.

People: The Madina population, mainly of the Tonko-Limba ethnic group, comprised people from many towns and villages. In fact, until recently, the town was called Madina Junction because it had developed at an intersection of several dirt roads. This central location made Madina the pulse throb of the whole Northeast Kambia District.

While the high-ranking rebels were usually of the Mende tribe even in Madina, the rank and file were from various tribes, with a good contingent of local Tonko-Limba element. The RUF had entrenched themselves in the town for the last three years. Slowly it seemed that the whole population of 5,000 had become their sympathizers and/or abettors. Perhaps that explains in part why the town of Madina was not razed or burned to the ground as Kambia had been. Yet, deep inside, not all Madina villagers agreed with the rebels. There were notable exceptions in the underground, whom we personally came to know as we received the confidence of so many who visited and talked to us. Regardless of the sympathy (or lack thereof) for the rebel movement, most people in town seemed to respect us. Many assisted us both in kind and with money, which, considering the abject constraints of these poor people, moved and inspired us.

Almost every day during the first month of our detention

we received "official" delegations from a number of surrounding villages, some as far as a three-hour walk through pathways in the forest. They came to express sympathy and solidarity, offer prayers, and bring a good supply of rice, fruit and chickens.

Usually the delegation—a cross-section of the population of from 10 to 40 people—was led by the catechist and the head-teacher of the Catholic grade school, followed by the village chief or speaker and at times even the Imam. The first group to come was from the tribal chief of Madina itself. The Paramount Chief (PC) of Madina had been murdered a couple of years earlier, so the delegation was headed by the regent chief and made up of a mixed group of friends and uncommitted individuals. All, however, sympathized with and encouraged us.

Typically a delegation from out of town would approach singing church songs or just drumming. They would meet us in the grass *buffer* (in West Africa a small, round, temporary grass roof supported by sticks as a protection from the sun) built just outside the Mission house. They would deposit their various gifts, such as bowls and bags, on the ground and then the catechist or teacher would introduce the head of the delegation, the chief, the Imam, and any personality present. During these formalities the crowd would settle down on the ground in and around the buffer, with the children struggling to get as close to Father Franco as possible. After the introduction the teacher or the chief would give a short speech, expressing their sorrow for finding us prisoners of the rebels and recalling for all to hear the many things the Catholic Mission had done for all the people of their village regardless of tribe, religion or social condition. Then they offered their gifts, tokens of their gratitude and solidarity.

Father Franco would then thank them and remind them that God does not allow things to happen for no reason. He explained, "Even our capture can be viewed as God's grace, for it brought the two of us back into your midst. It drew us close to you in prayer and allowed us to share their difficult time during this war." Then Father Franco would introduce me to his people. Although many of them already knew me, formalities of their culture required that I, who wasn't stationed there as parish priest, should be introduced. After Father Franco's thanking all for their thoughtfulness in visiting and in bringing gifts, anyone could talk and share comments. A very brief prayer session and more singing ended the visit and the visitors hastened to depart since the group had to reach their village before dark.

The generosity of these poor people enabled us to be generous ourselves with others who lived nearby and did not have enough to eat, especially village children and child soldiers. The end result was that the Mission house was often surrounded by the very poor, seeking help from us who had just received help!

Special Friends, Rebels and Non-Rebels: Among the many people showing us goodwill were a dozen or so who were particularly close and loyal to us because of religion, past employment, or a special relationship arising from assistance we'd given them during sickness, family deaths or rebels' amputations. These special friends, a dozen or so, included both rebels and non-rebels. It was with the help and assistance of some of them, albeit without their knowledge and/or direct cooperation, that we later engineered our escape. The risk of having our friends punished for complicity weighed heavily on us and it was one of the reasons we did not attempt to escape much sooner than we did.

Among these special friends were the four Mission boys Father Franco had left in charge of the Mission after he had been confined to Pamelap. They were high school students whose schooling was interrupted when the system broke down. Around them there was a small group of rebels and non-rebels, who were secretly relating news as well as rumors of interest to us.

Their faithfulness and support was a source of both encouragement and apprehension; the first because we knew we could count on them, the second because we realized the risk they were running if their spying was discovered. These friends often briefed us on the development of the war, movements of guerrillas, and particularly the big leaders such as Brigadier Nimalty Kargbo, Superman (Brigadier Dennis Mingo), Brigadier Brima Varney, Colonel Komba, and others of importance. We knew for a fact that some friendly rebels were worrying about us and actually shielded us from possible vicious attacks by ill-intentioned, cruel or drugged rebels.

One evening as I sat in a corner of the Mission compound

feeling somewhat dejected and discouraged because of all the destruction and loss, one of the friendly child soldiers, Mohamed who was about 14, passed by. Seeing my mournful face, he said in a chiding tone, "Oh, Father Victor, why are you always so sad? Don't you know we love you?" I looked up at him and said scornfully, "Oh, yeah, Mohamed, how do you love me?" He looked at me for a brief instant and then said, "You still have two hands, don't you?" I reflected for a moment on the hacking of limbs his question hinted at and then said, "Yes, of course. Thanks be to God and to you too, my friend."

David Yillah was another tremendous supporter. He was the ex-seminarian who had become one of the catechists of the church at Madina. Talented and charismatic with the young, a year before our arrival he had been "recruited" at gunpoint by the rebels to be the youth organizer of the town's young people who were not officially members of the movement. Although performing the duties assigned to him by the rebels, David loyally reported to us all he could see concerning the rebels' movements. He came around quite often, offering words of encouragement and assuring us that generally speaking there was no ill will toward us in the local leadership. It was the High Command in Makeni that was blocking our release in the hope of obtaining certain advantages by resolving our captivity.

Interpretation of Rumors and Events: Ever since that terrible day of our capture at Pamelap, our minds were constantly noting events, gathering rumors, interpreting situations, and comparing statements of various rebel personalities regarding us or the war in order to discover the meaning and consequences of our capture. Above and beyond the initial fear and the continuing danger inherent to being in the middle of a war, we did have an optimistic feeling (or perhaps an illusion?) that no deadly harm would come to us. This was primarily because of our personal relationship with the local high command of the rebels and the respect and friendliness they had shown to us. Yes, we were robbed of everything—both personal and Mission's belongings—and were effectively kept prisoners, but we did receive repeated signs of goodwill. Our optimism may have been naïve, especially considering what had happened to other missionaries (Fathers, Sisters and Brothers) killed by the rebels. Yet, we clung to this optimism, which was reinforced by the constant promise that we would be released "very soon."

However, with the passage of time, a good 15 days into our captivity, the optimism about our immediate release began to fade. We realized that we were there to stay and that the goodwill and promises voiced by our immediate captors were not shared by the high command in Makeni.

What plans did they have for us? Wouldn't one of our friends tell us something? As it turned out no one, not even among our closest friends, told us anything. Either they didn't really know anything or weren't willing to risk leaking certain information to us. It was in this frame of mind that we found ourselves engaged in all sorts of speculations about events, rumors and people near and far.

It was absolutely clear that our capture was not a prearranged plan. Neither was it an act of hostility toward our religion. In fact, quite the contrary. Several rebels even of high rank declared themselves proud to be Christian and even Catholic. Another clear feature was that the rebel command who had mounted the attack on Pamelap either overlooked the fact that we were in Pamelap during the attack or perhaps expected that we had had time to run just before or at the very beginning of the assault. This we deduced from the expression of surprise on their faces when we were brought before them. But then again, perhaps they did expect to capture us. If so they played the part well in acting surprised, shaking hands with us and even apologizing!

Another element in the puzzle that became clear at the outset and was reinforced during the first few days of our capture was that we—missionary Fathers, white men, highly respected and believable witnesses (especially with the international community)—had seen something that the RUF always denied: the Sierra Leone rebels had indeed invaded the Republic of Guinea. They went into Guinea either for the ideological reason of exporting their revolution into that country, or for the practical purpose of functioning as mercenaries for the Guinean rebels, at least in the initial stage of their revolution. Now that the war in Sierra Leone was winding down and the Sierra Leone rebels were expected to disarm, they could get rid of their expensive weapons while making good money in selling them to the Guineans.

During the assault on Pamelap the attackers must have been at least one thousand strong. The vast majority were clearly of the RUF, but there was a sprinkling of different nationalities. Over the shooting we could detect commands issued in Krio, Liberian, Burkinabe, Ivorian, and Guinean. Some slogans were shouted in French over fake radio transmitters to the effect that the Rassemblement des Forces Démocratiques de Guinée (RFDG)— the Guinean rebels—had come to overthrow President Lansana Conteh. However, the mimicking of the radio broadcast was rather naïve, in fact comical, since the units the rebels held were obviously unsuitable for transmitting anything. The villagers who were scrambling about in panic could hardly pay much attention to these antics anyway.

At the end of the second day of the attack, toward evening, four colonels—Joe, Ezekiel, Sandy, and Matthew—all friendly to us, stopped by for a short "consultation." They knew that we were aware of the "reasons of war" for holding us. In those days the United Nations had a team of observers in West Africa on a fact-finding mission about reported cross-border trespasses by the RUF into Liberia and Guinea.

Colonel Joe began, "Fathers, what shall we do? You know the situation. We cannot let you go. It would betray our movement." I said to them, "Look, we were not the only ones there. There were thousands of people who saw what happened; sooner or later the truth will come out even without our testimony. At any rate, if it will make you feel safer, we promise you that if you will release us we will avoid making any statement to the media about the happenings in Pamelap. We will simply say that we heard people broadcasting in French that they were Guinean rebels of the Rassemblement des Forces Démocratiques de Guinée come to overthrow President Lansana Conteh. In this way we will not compromise your dealings with the United Nations. We would never do anything to jeopardize the peace efforts in Sierra Leone."

We thought that this little speech would satisfy them, but apparently it did not. They said that they would discuss things with Brig. Brima Varney and let us know. We guessed that the real obstacle came not from the local leadership, but rather from the high command in Makeni, Gen. Jussu Kamara, Brig. Nimalty Kargbo, Colonel Jibril Massaquoi, Brig. Dennis Mingo (Superman) and others.

With the passage of time, it became clear to the whole world that indeed the RUF was responsible for raids into Guinea and Liberia. Yet even then the Sierra Leone rebels always officially denied any involvement with Guinea. By then new motives came to bear for holding us captive. We learned this from secret information we obtained from rebel friends. We had become, or so the high command believed, valuable pawns in its dealings with the Sierra Leone government, the international community, and the UN. We had become bargaining chips for exchange of RUF prisoners, money or goods.

Another reason, as mentioned, was to entice us into voluntarily staying with them and functioning as religious leaders, organizing church services and school and social activities. Thus the idea would be projected that the RUF was a humane and socially conscious movement, bent on the development and welfare of the citizens.

So, perhaps, we were kept as hostages for several different, though conflicting, purposes. Or maybe this was only in our minds, thus showing the quandary we were in, trying to guess and construe the many variables of the situation.

The longer our detention, the greater was our apprehension on account of the many setbacks the rebels were sustaining on multiple fronts, both militarily and diplomatically. It became clear that the RUF was splitting into two quite distinct groups. One was the RUF peace-negotiating main front, which was hammering out a new peace treaty with the government and the UNAMSIL. This group, under the direction of General Jussu Kamara, who had become overall field commander of all the RUF in the country, represented the majority of the rebels, who had lost hope of military victory and were tired of fighting.

The other, smaller group, were those who were still actively involved with the revolution in Guinea by contributing fighting personnel, weapons and logistics. We came to know that this front had been placed under the direct command of Brig. Gen. Nimalty Kargbo. The guerrillas at his disposal were hardened in the rebellion and still all fired up to continue the fighting, if not in Sierra Leone, then in Guinea. Apparently this group acted almost as a separate unit, independently of the diplomatic front directed by Gen. Jussu Kamara.

Unfortunately, because of the geographical position of Madina and Kamaqui so close to the Guinean border, the RUF contingent pushing the fight into Guinea under Brig. Gen. Nimalty Kargbo had its headquarters in this area and we fell under his direct command. This may explain why, according to secret information received from our rebel friends, Bishop George Biguzzi, had repeatedly contacted Gen. Jussu Kamara and obtained from him firm promises that we would be released. Yet nothing ever happened. It became clear in our minds that the rebels were not acting any longer under one command and we were under the authority of a splinter group, a bête noir worse than the official RUF.

Our friends among the rebel leaders became embarrassed to visit us and we gradually came to realize that even when they passed by the Mission compound they avoided stopping to talk with us. We came to know of their presence only from secret information we got from our friendly child-soldiers.

The talks and the progress toward peace sponsored by the "official" RUF led by Gen. Jussu Kamara caused a constant flow of civilians among the various areas in Sierra Leone. Many people began moving to and from Freetown in an atmosphere of openness and exchange. Thus we were able to receive, always in secret, small packages of food and necessities from the Fathers in Freetown. We even exchanged some scribbled notes.

This correspondence confirmed what we had already surmised from several reports from the rank-and-file rebels in Madina. The revolution in Guinea was going badly for the Sierra Leone rebels who were sustaining terrible losses of personnel and ground positions. Whatever advantages they had obtained in the first month of the fighting were now being reversed with terrible pounding from the Guinean army.

The unpredictable consequences of our being in rebel hands always loomed over us, but we decided to bear it since we could provide Christian witness even under such conditions. Then out of nowhere something happened that changed our outlook and precipitated our decision to flee.

CHAPTER THIRTEEN

A Threat and a Plan

Unexpected Developments

On the evening of Thursday, Nov. 3, 2000, shortly after prayers, we were sitting in the dark outside the Mission talking with the usual cluster of churchgoers, mostly children. A couple of child soldiers who were good friends of ours and very close to the rebel command (in fact one of them was the son of a colonel) approached us with an air of immediacy and secrecy. They urgently signaled that they wanted to talk to us privately. Excusing ourselves from the group, we went inside. It was already dark and we purposely left the lantern outside the house, so that we could see anyone coming, going, or stopping at the door, while remaining hidden ourselves in the dark.

Momodu whispered, "Father Franco, we overheard a conversation in the command post that orders came from the high command in Makeni that the two of you should be turned over to the Guinean rebels on the other side of the border. We do not know the time, but it would seem that this will be done in the near future." I asked, "What for?" The boys had not learned the reasons for this decision, but they were clearly not happy with it. In fact, they appeared quite worried for our safety. Father

Franco, who knew our informants better than I, thanked them profusely for their solidarity and friendship. He then suggested that they keep their ears open for any additional information while we ourselves would try to tactfully investigate with some of the higher-ups stationed in Madina, without compromising the boys. We returned quickly to the group outside in order not to arouse their suspicion or curiosity.

After closing down for the night, we whispered our impressions of the new information. Why would they want to turn us over to the Guineans? Nothing was happening without a reason. There had to be an angle. We evaluated various hypotheses and figured that, probably, our captors were trying to kill two birds with one stone: blame our capture on the Guineans and make some money in the process.

We had become a very inconvenient prize in their hands. The international community was pressing for our release. Although the rebels wouldn't admit to the world that they had captured us, they couldn't deny that we were now in their hands. Perhaps they thought they could turn us over to the Guineans and then say, "See, we told you we did not capture these missionaries; the Guinean rebels in Pamelap did! We only protected them for a time but then the Guineans came to get them back."

In addition to getting rid of us, the RUF would receive some good money from the Guineans, who in turn were hoping to recoup it many times over by the ransom paid by the Catholic

Mission, some foreign governments, or anyone who wanted to redeem us. In this deal both the RUF and the Guinean rebels would profit. It was late that night when we stopped considering this matter, with the understanding that we would discuss it further the next day.

Two days later I was sitting at the back of the Mission house, where I usually took refuge to enjoy some privacy and quiet while reading and praying. Father Franco sent for me. "Come quickly. There's an interesting visitor!" I closed my book and went directly to the front room where Father Franco usually sat receiving all kinds of visitors—men, women and children, both village people, chiefs, rank-and-file rebels and commanders. I always admired Father Franco's infinite patience in interacting with people from morning till night. As for me, oftentimes I couldn't take it any longer and retreated to the back of the house which had an exit into a quiet cassava (manioca) and ground-nut (peanut) garden.

Sitting with Father Franco were three people: a middle-aged man in military fatigues but unarmed and two men in their late teens clad in rough civilian clothes and shouldering AK-47 rifles— obviously RUF rebels, whom we'd never seen before. Upon my entering the room the military man in fatigues stood up and, extending his hand, introduced himself in correct English, albeit with a Guinean/French accent, "I am Sekou Souaré Kourouma, president of the RFDG. I have come to you with a proposal concerning your liberation."

After a brief exchange of pleasantries, he sat down and he continued, "We all agree that you, men of God, should not be held prisoners. So we of the RFDG, in conjunction with our comrades of the RUF, have worked out a plan for your liberation. Since this part of Sierra Leone is still enmeshed in war, the safest way to release you would be through Guinea. The plan was devised that you could be transferred into our custody and we in turn would be happy to release you to any nearby country of your choice, excluding Sierra Leone and Guinea. How do you feel about this plan?"

Naturally, given the information of two nights before, this proposal did not come to us as news, but we were stunned by the fast pace of events. Father Franco politely and diplomatically stated that we were surprised by this turn of events and needed time to consider all the implications. How would we be released? How were we to travel to a third country that was not Sierra Leone or Guinea? This much Father spoke openly. But he later told me his apprehensions: Why couldn't the RUF take us to the Liberian border and free us there into the hands of the Liberian government that was sponsoring every movement of the RUF? Why had none of our friends in the RUF command in Madina ever mentioned this alternative? With these and similar thoughts, both Father Franco and I tried to get as much insight into this plan from this seemingly well-disposed president of the RFDG. We doubted, in fact, that he actually was a president of anything, but did not let on and referred to him as "Mr. President."

Mr. Kourouma parried all the questions as best he could, always in a kind, but almost condescending manner. He said that "reasons of war" (again) prevented the RUF from taking direct action in our regard. The choice of where to go, following our liberation, would be exclusively up to us, and modalities could be worked out to our complete satisfaction and safety. If we accepted the plan, we would walk across the Guinean border escorted by the RFDG and repair to one of the RUF camps. From there it would be arranged to have a helicopter take us to an international airport in any bordering country. He assured us that he had discussed all aspects of this plan with the RUF High Command; in fact, should we accept this plan, he would proceed directly to Makeni to finalize all arrangements.

It became obvious to us that the request for our assent to this plan was a pure formality, or worse, a cover-up for something more sinister. Of course, we could not say that. So instead we expressed gratitude for "Mr. President's" interest in our liberation and assured him that we would cooperate with any effort to set us free. This kind of talk seemed to please the man. He stood up and, taking leave, promised to return soon with more definitive information regarding our "release." The two bodyguards showed no feelings or emotion; nor did they respond to our farewells.

As soon as they left, we began evaluating this visit and comparing it with the information we had received the night before. Was this a positive development or was it a treacherous snare? We were not sure which, but considering the proverbial deviousness of the RUF, the likelihood was that this plan was rather fishy! *"Timeo Danaos et dona ferentes"* (I mistrust the Greeks, even when bringing gifts), said I. The reference was to the stratagem used by the Greeks who, while seemingly abandoning the siege of Troy, left on its shores a gigantic wooden horse, purportedly as a gift to the gods. In fact, it contained warriors who, during the night while the Trojans were celebrating the withdrawal of the enemy, attacked and burned the city.

Somehow we had to know more. We asked several rebel friends, people who should have been in the know, but got nowhere. Again, either they didn't know or were afraid to talk. We resigned ourselves to watching what developed. We were not at all reassured because the movement of arms and personnel all around us seemed to be intensifying. The RUF was split and the two of us in Madina were trapped on the wrong side of the fence.

Three weeks went by and our quandary remained unresolved. Without warning, another unexpected event precipitated our worst fears. On Thursday, Nov. 30, we had a totally unexpected visit from one Colonel Sheriff, the commanding officer in charge of the Kamaquie rebel post, 55 miles northeast of Madina. (He was the same Sheriff who, as only a captain the year before, took me from Kamaquie to the Sierra Leone-Guinea border to set me free.) Colonel Sheriff arrived with a Land Rover and entered the house with a beautiful smile. After the conventional pleasantries, he said, "Fathers, I bring you great news!"

The deviousness of the RUF was sometimes very subtle, but at times rather crass. This time, we thought, it seemed crass. He said, "Fathers, Christmas is approaching, and we at Kamaquie thought that it would be nice to have you two celebrate Christmas in our church. As you know, I myself am a fervent Catholic. Wouldn't you like to join us for this occasion? We have very nice accommodations for you there, and the people would be so glad to see you among us!" Father Franco thanked him for the proposal, but pointed out that we already had a church right here in Madina, with a very well organized congregation. It wouldn't be correct to abandon this flock in order to go to another. At most we could share the priests, one Father in Madina and one in Kamaquie.

Colonel Sheriff did not seem happy with this counterproposal, but did not refuse it outright. However, the conclusion of the conversation was disconcerting. He said that he was on his way to Rokupr (34 miles southwest of Madina) to confer with Brig. Gen. Brima Varney. Upon his return in four or five days, he would pick us up for Kamaquie! His "proposal" had simply been a polite way of saying that we should get ready to go, whether we liked it or not. Father Franco's counterproposal was not even considered. Then the scheme became clear to us: Kamaquie was the center of the RUF—RFDG exchange and war planning. Our being there would've been the first step in turning us over to the Guinean rebels in a smooth and easy way.

The Decision

As soon as the colonel left, Father Franco said, "This is it. It's time we cut loose. Do you think your back can sustain the run?"

I replied, "I think so. Anyway, we have no choice." To reduce the possibility that our decision could leak out by having more people involved in the planning, and recognizing that Father Franco had the best knowledge of the place and the people there, I added, "Yes, Franco, let's go. You alone do the planning. Anything you arrange is fine with me." He answered, "Agreed. I'll try to plan for Sunday night. I'll keep you posted; stand ready."

The next morning, Friday, Father Franco informed me that he was going to set up some diversionary tactics, in order to deflect any possible suspicion. He sent word to the town chief, to the rebels' police quarters, and to Colonel Arbourt, that he would like to take them to the present site of the Catholic Grade School to explain a plan for expanding it. This was a project already formed several years earlier, even before the rebel takeover, and was then suspended because of the war. Now Father Franco used it to create the impression that not only were we committed to remaining with the rebels but wanted even to expand our work. This would please them immensely as they always tried to entice us to cooperate with their leadership. And nothing would assure them more that we were not planning an escape. Father Franco knew their psychology well!

The Plan and Immediate Preparations

On the evening of Saturday, Dec. 2, Father Franco unfolded the master plan of the escape. By midnight between Dec. 3 and Dec. 4, the new moon would provide a night of total darkness. We would have to make our way stealthily through the rebels' huts, houses, and posts that totally surrounded the Mission and were scattered throughout the whole town. Father capitalized on the fact that it was *Armattan* season, a three-month period in West Africa from about the end of November to the end of February when night temperature drops to the lower 60's, decidedly very cold by tropical standards. That meant that all rebels not actively engaged in fighting would be inside their huts, clustered around a sparkling fire and wrapped in blankets.

The ground plan was to go around the ammunition depot, which was right behind the Mission, and then slowly zigzag down the center of town, around and behind the grade school and toward the main checkpoint manned by the rebels. This was located on a dirt road that entered the town from the direction of Kambia. The checkpoint was the most dangerous spot, since warriors there were on the alert 24 hours a day.

We were to cross the dirt road some 150 yards south of the checkpoint and then disappear straight into the thick bush. Going in a southeasterly direction would put us on the way toward the Sanda-Mabolonto region, a zone patrolled by the United Nations peacekeeping force. There, beyond the Maboleh River, the last of three rivers we were to cross, we would be out of rebels' reach. The plan called for walking two nights and two days at a pace as fast as a terrain obstructed by forests, swamps, rivers, and hills would permit. We were always to choose solitary or abandoned footpaths rather than beaten tracks, in order to avoid unpleasant and dangerous encounters. However, we were always to keep within the general environs of towns and villages that Father Franco knew quite well and from which we could expect some help, should we need it.

In this plan there was only one rendezvous, which had to be prearranged: the crossing of the Little Scarcies River, which ran southwesterly and divided the Kambia District from the Port Loko District. The Little Scarcies was a mighty river that couldn't be waded. Father Franco could probably swim it, but I, with my recent back injury, certainly could not have done it. Besides, its width at the point we had to cross it was about 100 yards, and the waters were perilous and crocodile infested. We needed a boat and someone to ferry us across. This could be done only at night, for the whole length and breadth of this watercourse was well visible from both sides. Father Franco, through the cooperation of a close friend of Madina, arranged the rendezvous for 4:30 a.m. Monday, Dec. 4.

After we crossed the Little Scarcies, at the first opportunity in any of the local villages we would dispatch a messenger by bicycle to intercept the closest United Nations patrol on the other side of the Maboleh River. The message was to be written on a small paper wrapped in plastic and was to read, "The Fathers from Madina Tonko have escaped. Please meet them at Barmoi-Kassi and radio Bishop George Biguzzi in Freetown about this operation." We wouldn't be on safe ground until we crossed the Maboleh River some 40 miles away. Secrecy was of the utmost importance. That's why I willingly let Father Franco handle it all alone. I had given him the $900 I was able to save the time we were captured.

Only two people knew about the escape. One was a close friend of Father Franco, Anthony Rogers, a local young man in his twenties. He was an amateur photographer, who, although not a member of the movement, served the rebels with his photography. He always carried in his bag a small, automatic camera. Anthony had decided long before to leave Madina with his family, whom he had sent ahead to Freetown weeks before these events. He was to accompany us throughout the escape and was to arrange for a canoe and a boatman at the Little Scarcies River. The second was Paul (nicknamed Lala), a small village boy whom Father also knew quite well. His job was to go out around 11 p.m. to midnight on the night of our escape and scout the path we were to follow, making sure that no one was still prowling or walking around. Then he was to lead us on this path from the Mission to just out of the town of Madina, after which he was to return quietly to his own home, without letting even his family know his part in the plan.

No one else knew about the plan, not even our closest friends, the Mission boys, or the catechist. We decided to keep everyone out of the picture to reduce as much as possible the danger of reprisals after our escape.

Reprisals were to occur anyway, but fortunately not to the extent they might have. Father Franco wrote a long open letter, addressed to the leaders and the rank-and-file RUF rebels. The letter was to be left on the altar, and was to be found the morning of the escape, at the 7 a.m. Mass time. The gist of the letter was as follows:

"We, the Fathers, have decided to leave you because we finally understood that you only wanted to exploit our case. You had been promising us for three months that you would free us, but you never kept your promise. We want to go, not to abandon you but in order to return at a better time and to extend to you and the rest of the population our help and assistance. By being confined here in Madina, cut off from our resources, we cannot render you the help we could and want to give. So we will go, but only to return to you. Please do not blame or hold anyone around here responsible for our escape. Nobody of the people here knew of this. Nobody of the rebels or of the population knew or helped us to escape. We did it all by ourselves. You are aware that after so many years we know our way around this part of the country better than you do. Goodbye and God bless you."

Sunday, Dec. 3 was the feast day of the patron Saint of our Missionary Society, St. Francis Xavier. Father Franco warned me that in order to dispel any possible suspicion we were to behave as if we were actually planning the normal activities for the following week. Consequently after Mass, well attended as usual, he announced the church calendar for the following week: the time of daily Mass, of the Rosary, and of night prayers, the timetable for cleaning the church, choir practice in preparation for the Christmas Novena, as well as preparation for the lectors and choir practice for the following Sunday.

We spent the rest of the day preparing for the breakaway. As always we were aware that, even among so many friends and sympathizers, there could be eyes trained on us at all times. Every movement was to be done very carefully in order to avoid creating any suspicion of anything afoot.

One very important thing was to devise some way to conceal the color of the skin of our face and hands during the run. At night the color of a white man's skin shows up quite conspicuously, especially to the Africans with their sharp night vision. In general, no one in Sierra Leone would be particularly surprised to see people walking around or passing by at night. But a white man would be spotted right away and was bound to attract attention and curiosity, if not outright suspicion.

At midday on Saturday I called Ahmidu, a young boy who oftentimes came around the Mission, and, with a flimsy excuse of some service he had rendered me a few days earlier, I offered to buy him a hat. So off we went to the town market near the Mission where all kinds of goods were neatly arranged on the ground over mats and plastic sheets, divided by kind and ownership. We went to the *"congo"* clothes (used clothes) area, and I picked out for the boy a nice black winter hat equipped with flaps that could be drawn over the ears and neck. That hat was perfect for me to hide my gray hair and white skin and beard. Wearing that, with a dark long sleeved shirt and black pants and with hands stuffed in my pockets, I could pass, on a moonless night, like a barely visible shadow.

I asked Ahmidu, "Do you like this?" He said, "Oh, yes, this will keep me warm now that it is so cold during the Armattan." "Try it on," I said. He put it on and expressed satisfaction. I said, "Let's buy a spare one for someone in your family." The boy proudly wore the hat all the way back to the Mission.

Arriving at the house, I asked Ahmidu, "Can I keep your spare hat for tonight?" "Of course Father," he said. "Thank you then," I said. " I'll see you tomorrow." Off he went, very happy and, I guessed, surprised at my generosity in getting him two hats. I felt guilty about cheating him of his spare one.

My footwear was a pair of black plastic sandals over black socks. Father Franco chose to shroud himself in a long black shawl that completely covered his head, shoulders, arms, and hands. He looked like an old woman, another shadow in a moonless night. Of course, we knew that even with all these precautions, if we came face to face with any rebel, we would be finished. This would happen if we bumped into them on the same path, or if the quick beam of a flashlight or the glimmer of a bonfire from a distance revealed our white skin. This latter event we hoped to minimize by our garb. We prayed, as the moment of our escape drew near.

CHAPTER FOURTEEN

The Escape

After night prayers on Sunday evening, Dec. 3, we spend time in front of the Mission, chatting with the usual crowd of mostly children. We want to scrupulously stick to the routine. At around 9:30, as usual, we took leave of our friends as if to retire for the night. The moon is still visible, but on its way down; and the Armattan wind, like a cool breeze (cold, for the Africans), is gently blowing. Voices all around have dwindled. Some conversations of people and rebels can still be heard as they chat and bivouac. Inside the Mission we decide to let the lanterns burn until 10:30, the time when we usually put them out and go to sleep

Father Franco finishes the letter to the rebels. I step into another room where there is no lantern and look out the window towards the ammunition depot, which is also Capt. Kelvin's house. He is the head of the guards who are responsible for watching us. They are still on the veranda, chatting. I feel sorry for him and his comrades, as they would certainly be blamed for our escape. Capt. Kelvin is a friendly and trusting young man in his mid twenties. How can such seemingly good people get involved with a murderous bunch like the RUF? Oh, the mysteries and contradictions of the human heart and the influence of the environment!

At 10:30 we put out both lanterns. Now we are in absolute darkness. We do have flashlights, but we dare not point them anywhere, except now and then and only straight at the floor, so as not to bump into doors and furniture. Father Franco goes to unlock the front door and leave it ajar. Little Paul is expected to come in to tell us how our escape route through the village looked. Also, Anthony, who has arranged for the canoe to cross the Little Scarcies, should be returning any minute now.

Father Franco, slowly feeling his way around in the darkness, approaches me and touches my backpack. "No, no," he whispers, "It's too encumbering, too big. You'd better reduce it." He is right; I myself was feeling uncertain when I packed it. Returning to my room, I decide to leave behind the backpack altogether. It contains two prayer books, some toiletries, one change of clothes, a pen, pencil and a couple of notebooks full of notes from the books I have read during the past months of restricted movements. The pack is actually rather small, but considering that we are about to run for a good 40 miles, I conclude that even a small weight could be too much. Father Franco is right, and subsequent developments abundantly will prove it. I only take the two notebooks out of the bag, wrap them in clear plastic and stuff them inside my pants, under my belt. The rest I let go. Now my legs will only have to carry the weight of my body. Heavy enough at 185 pounds!

Feeling my way back to the entrance, I hear whispering. Anthony is there and asks me in a whisper how I feel and if I am ready to go. He confides, always in whispers, "Father, I've got a bicycle at Laia (the first village we are expected to reach), and from there I can give you a ride for a good stretch, until we reach the first swamp." This, of course, is in consideration of my back injury. I thank him for the unexpected thoughtfulness, which Father Franco himself may have suggested. I tell him that it is not necessary to go to that extent, but if that has been planned, OK.

At that point Paul enters. He assures us that all is quiet in town and that all people are inside their huts, except at the checkpoint. In fact, we can hear voices coming from that direction. Paul says, "A big truck of rebels is stuck right in the middle of the road in front of the checkpoint. They are having engine problems, and they've sent for Olah the fitter."

"Good," Franco whispers. "That will divert their attention from us when we have to cross the road there. Let's move." The luminous dial of my watch marks 12:30 a.m. Franco closes the front door; the Mission boys have all the Mission's keys. We exit the back door into the inner court of the compound. We cross it very carefully, without making a sound, occasionally lighting the ground between our feet with the flashlight. The Mission boys are sleeping in three rooms flanking the inner court, and we don't want to alert them as we pass. We enter the back of the church. There on the altar, Father Franco places the letter to the rebels, using a candlestick stand to hold it in place. The catechist, David Yillah, will find it when he comes for the 7 a.m. Mass. We head for the main entrance of the church and exit into the town.

Darkness is total. We have already been in darkness for more than two hours inside the house. I hoped that by now I would have gotten used to it and at least be able to make out shapes. But I can see nothing, not a thing! The flashlight is in my hand, but I dare not use it.

I feel for Paul's hand and grab it, whispering, "Let me follow right behind you. Please, hold my hand." He answers, "Yes, Father, hold onto me. I can see enough." We proceed in single file: first Father Franco, then Anthony, then Paul and myself. It is imperative that we avoid any noise, especially foot shuffling. We are threading our way down very narrow paths between huts, sometimes within inches of doors and windows.

Suddenly we all stop in our tracks. Ahead of us someone has come out of the hut...to pee. How anyone could spot a shadow in that darkness beats me. After a few seconds we resume walking but change direction. The unexpected course takes us right in front of the ammunition depot and Capt. Kelvin's house. A terrible moment. That is the very place where the guards who should be watching us are staying. Thank God for the Armattan breeze!

After a few minutes we pass the depot and the four houses in line with it. At that point we leave the dirt road and cut into the savanna behind the houses, toward our school. I breathe a sigh of relief. But, having abandoned the beaten path, walking in darkness becomes more dangerous because of the rough terrain, which not only makes it easy to stumble but also causes a lot of foot shuffling. However, for a 15-minute period we are not surrounded by huts and so feel somewhat safer.

Now we are directly behind the Catholic Primary (Grade) School. About 300 feet beyond the school we pass the latrine pits. Then about 250 yards farther, we are at the main road, 150 yards south of the rebels' checkpoint, where the truck is stalled. We pause on the side of the road, crouching in the high grass. We can easily hear the rebels' voices and see the shape of the truck silhouetted against its headlights and the glimmer of a campfire. Facing north, away from us, it blocks the whole road right in front of the checkpoint. The rebels seem to be busy repairing or changing tires, with the fussing and boisterous shouting typical of African road emergencies. This is good for us, since the din they are making is reducing their alertness and will cover any noise we will have to make in crossing the road. One at a time we take five quick leaps and clear the road disappearing into the thick, high bushes east of it. Once we have all crossed, while still crouching in the grass, we listen momentarily to the voices at the checkpoint. There is no change in pattern; they haven't spotted us.

Father Franco, speaking for the first time since we left, whispers, "All OK. Let's go. Follow me." Again we move in single file. There is no road and the steps are difficult, but pretty soon we reach a footpath. We stop there and Father Franco whispers again, "Now we can continue at a more relaxed pace and use the flashlight, but only to point down around our feet, never up or anywhere else."

At this point we advise Paul Lala to return to town. He is still at home in this environment here, and we don't want him to go into unfamiliar territory. Our plan calls for him to only accompany us until we clear Madina. We thank him and Father Franco gives him some little money as a token of gratitude. As Lala turns back, we continue on.

Two miles down the footpath we come to the first village, Laia of the Kambia District (different from a later Laia in the Port Loko District). It is now 1:15 a.m. All is quiet, not a living soul around except for goats and ducks sleeping next to the huts. Just as we are about to leave the village behind us, Anthony says to us, "Fathers, stop here. Wait a moment for me." He disappears into the darkness. In a few minutes, which seem hours, he returns with a bicycle he had left there in a hidden place the previous day. "Here, Father Victor, sit on the luggage rack and keep your legs spread out." I heartily thank him, even though I see right away that this won't work.

Sitting on a bicycle luggage rack on a bumpy dirt path is not comfortable, but this is the least of the problems. What really becomes difficult is the strain of keeping my legs spread out while my back is jouncing up and down. It soon becomes unbearable. "Anthony, my friend, I'm sorry but I can't endure this. My back hurts more than if I were running. Please stop. I will walk. I think I can make it all right." I thank him for his kindness and thoughtfulness.

Anthony is a very smart man. He understands, stops, lets me down, and says, "OK, Father, if you can walk, that will be better for me too." We continue at a lively pace on foot, he holding onto the bicycle and the two of us behind him. The darkness is still heavy, but the footpath presents little or no obstacles and we can make good time.

The next village is Kanyatara. Again, nobody is in sight, only sleeping sheep and goats. Just past the town, Anthony says to the two of us, "Please wait here. I am going for the boatman." He disappears again, walking his bicycle that he intends to leave in his friend's house. We wait for about 10 minutes. It's 2 a.m. The place is absolutely quiet with only the nocturnal animals of the forest exchanging calls. Father Franco asks in a whisper how I feel. I tell him that I am surprised to find myself in quite a good form, with no pain and no tiredness. Presently the shadows of three men silently approach.

It's Anthony and two villagers, one of whom is the owner of the boat, Jumu. He had arrived to this village the day before in order to meet us here now. The other is a friend, Momodu, the owner of the house where Jumu stayed overnight. We shake hands, whispering greetings, and then Father Franco and the boatman discuss briefly the itinerary to reach the Little Scarcies River at Kakonki, about 15 miles away. Both our new companions suggest that we abandon the beaten path, which would take us through Kabailor, Kasasi, and other villages. The chance of meeting some rebels or their sympathizers in those villages is very real and could compromise the whole venture. We agree, but propose that we do not depart too far from the footpath so as not to lose our way. We also want to be close to help in case of any emergency, such as an attack by wild animals.

Now the going becomes more challenging. Traveling off the footpath in total darkness means encountering all sorts of unseen obstacles. Fortunately we can now use our flashlight at will. Still, this part of the journey out in the wild becomes more and more difficult because of the rough terrain, the stumbling, and the sustained pace of the march.

The stretch of about nine miles from the Kasasi area to Kakonki by the Little Scarcies is made up of three swamps intersected by two small rivers. When we picked up Jumu and Momodu at Kaniatara, I thought we were quite close to the Little Scarcies, but now, after trampling and splashing for about an hour, I realize that I had misjudged the distance and timing. At one point I ask Momodu, "How far is the Little Scarcies?" He says, "Oh, it's not too far, Father. We're almost there." I draw a sigh of relief, which is soon followed by the realization that for our Sierra Leonean forest people, time and distance are very relative concepts. "Just over there," or "far-far place," oftentimes mean the same thing. The end result is that you never know until you get there. In the meantime I fall flat on my face time after time, landing in mud, getting up, trampling, and splashing again and again.

The surprising thing to me is that while I am tiring, in fact by now almost exhausted, I have no back pain, which was what I had been dreading the most before we started this adventure. Thanks be to God for that. We now find ourselves by a river. I know that this is not the big one because everyone proceeds to strip to his underwear (those who have underwear) and gingerly enter the water. At first I say to myself, "What sense is there to undress? I'm already drenched and muddy! Actually, dunking into fresh, clean water will be cleansing and refreshing." But then I realize that I have my notebooks stuck under my belt and even though wrapped in plastic, immersion would ruin them. I quickly do as the others. I undress, put the bundle of clothes with the notebooks on my head, and go into the river. At one point the water almost reaches my chin, but by then I'm on the other side. A few more steps and out I come. What a cool and invigorating experience! But there's no time to relish the pleasure. We silently hurry into our clothes and on we trudge.

Soon I fall flat on my face again in the mud. The problem is that the terrain continually varies, and in the dark, with water everywhere, you can't avoid putting your foot in the wrong spot. Three times you catch your balance, but the fourth time you simply lose your bearings and down you go. I am relieved that this is happening more or less to the others as well, not just to me.

Now, another river, wading again. When we are all safely

on the other side, Jumu, the boatman, says, "Now you continue on in this direction to Kakonki, the village and the shore of the river where you will embark are down there." He points south and continues, "At the village don't take the footpath leading to the river. Continue straight south through the bush. You will come to a steep slope at the riverside; wait there for me. I am going this other way to retrieve the boat, which lies hidden in a safe bay. I will meet you at the bank coming up river with my boat." With that, off he goes.

The rest of us, with Momodu at the head, continue south. After about 15 minutes of more trudging and bumping into trees and stumps, the vegetation is becoming even thicker and more difficult to walk through. Suddenly we burst into a small clearing: Kakonki village. A few huts sit around the clearing. A spent fire pit is in the center and a footpath to the right. As per instructions we do not follow that, but instead dive into the thick bush again and in less than 10 minutes we come to a steep slope, which had been cleared of vegetation.

At last we have reached the Little Scarcies, flowing majestically. It is called "Little" not because it is small, but only to differentiate it from the "Big Scarcies," which is generally wider and, for a short stretch, runs parallel to the Littler Scarcies, some 30 miles away. We see the water only when we point our flashlights, but we can hear the murmuring of the current. On the other side is the Port Loko District: theoretically not RUF territory. Rebels, however, are known to disregard borders and trespass. Consequently it's never too safe, especially if we are being chased, which is a distinct possibility. Anyway, thanks be to God for coming safely this far.

We stop on the brow of a sharp 45-degree slope. The riverbank sits 50 feet below us. Inspecting it with the flashlight, we see no level ground by the waterside; so we stay at the top and wait. It is exactly 4:35 a.m. I am exhausted and from the sighs and behavior of the others, I understand that they too are tired. Two sit down on the muddy ground and one lies flat, full length, on branches. I stand, not because I feel strong, but because I know from experience of other long marches that sitting down before reaching the end would kill my remaining endurance.

Momodu explains in a subdued voice, "The boat is hidden half a mile downstream in a covered inlet of the river. We have to hide it, or the rebels would force us to use it for them, or take it from our hands altogether. We have hidden it for two years now and use it only when we are absolutely sure that no rebel is around." He continues pointing north, "Over there, very close to Kakonki, we have two other boats anchored alongside the river. Both are too damaged to be used, but as long as we keep them there, the rebels believe that's all we have got and will not harass us. Of course, someone could spy on us and then we'd be finished. So far we've been lucky."

After about 15 minutes we see a light coming toward us on the river. It is our boat coming up against the current and slowly approaching our position in the slope. With our flashlight we can now see the kind of boat Jumu has. Typical of those produced locally, it is a huge tree trunk, expertly carved, properly seasoned, and spacious enough for eight people. The challenge is to climb inside this type of boat and then keep your balance as you settle in. Though both Father Franco and I are used to these boats, they can still be tricky.

The boatman stops right in front of us. Raising his voice, he warns, "Be careful as you come down to the water's edge. The slope is steep and slippery and the bank gives straightaway to very deep waters, with no foothold. Be careful. Help yourselves down by hanging onto the bush branches lining either edge of the incline." Father Franco goes first. He hangs onto nearby branches while descending. As he reaches the water line and lifts his right foot to get into the boat, he lets go of the branch he was hanging onto. Too soon. Either his left foot slips or the muddy ground under it gives way, and his right foot pushes the boat out. He clings to the side of the boat, tipping it. One more inch and the boat will be swamped and capsize. Everyone looks on helplessly, while the boatman tries to counterbalance the rig with his own weight saying, "Careful, careful!" Thankfully, by a desperate effort of arm muscles, Father Franco succeeds in catapulting himself into the boat. Thanks be to God.

Then it is my turn. Having witnessed what had just happened, I lower myself with extreme caution, holding on to one branch after another. At the bottom I hold onto and lean on the last branch for support while I step into the boat. Only when safely in, I let the branch go.

Anthony and Momodu follow in the same manner. Jumu asks everyone to keep balance by sitting as still as possible to avoid any sudden shifting of weight. The slow rowing begins. All flashlights are off lest anyone see us from either bank as we push into the open. Even though the other side is not RUF territory, it is still dangerous.

It is almost 5 a.m. but still pitch dark. In the tropics, close to the equator, dawn is a quick affair: in five to 10 minutes it's almost full daylight. We remain in total silence throughout the 15-minute crossing. The rowing is laborious; the current is strong and keeps pushing the boat off course.

Disembarking is much easier than boarding. The water on this side is shallow and the bank mildly inclined. Jumu and Momodu helped by Anthony draw the boat right inside nearby bushes, remove the oars, and join us in getting up the bank toward the village of Mahoini, some 10 minutes away. Now morning light starts filtering through the fog of the forest. For the first time I begin to sense pain down my left leg. I don't pay much attention to it. I am tired. We decide to take a break at Mahoini.

We arrive just minutes past 6 a.m. We find the village people around a huge bonfire. It is almost a ritual for African villagers to build a big fire in the early morning in a safe, open space close to their huts, especially during Armattan season. Almost all the village people gather around it, both to get warm and to wake up. As we approach the fire, Jumu, evidently well known to those people, introduces us in general terms: two missionary Fathers escaping from the rebels. Space is immediately made available for us to sit by the fire. The traditional hospitality of these poor people prompts someone to quickly fetch two straw mats, so that Father Franco and I can lie down and rest. They offer us food in the form of roasted cassava, potatoes, and bananas. We thank them warmly but politely decline. Father Franco drinks some water. It feels so refreshing to be able to lie down by the fire while children run about laughing and playing, and adults exchange remarks about the rebels' situation.

Time goes fast. We realize that it is almost 7:30 a.m., the time when our escape should be discovered back in Madina, unless it had been found out earlier. Even though we have passed into the Port Loko District, we are still not completely out of rebels' reach. We must go for another 20 or 25 miles and cross the Mabole River before we will be in UN territory.

Father Franco talks with Momodu and Jumu, telling them we must continue on with some urgency. After many thanks and proper compensation, we part. Jumu and Momodu return to the river, and Father Franco, Anthony and I take the path toward Gbereh. From now on we will travel on beaten tracks.

Here begins my physical Calvary. I am feeling spasms in my left leg and a wicked sharp pain in my knee. At first I discount the pain as a natural consequence of the four hours spent trotting, stumping, and splashing in the forest and swamps. I look around and find myself a walking stick, the kind people back home, in northern Italy use when walking in alpine territory. They call it an *"alpenstock."* It is a slender, light stick strong enough to sustain your weight and slightly taller than your head. With the stick parallel to your body, you grasp it at shoulder's height, like a shepherd's or pilgrim's staff, and you slightly lean on it to accompany your stride forward. Several times in past years I walked up to 20 hours in a single day with the help of an alpenstock.

I'm hoping that the walking stick will help me along, but I am lagging behind and the pain is getting more intense. I wonder what it might be. I have never experienced such a problem in the past. This is not a cramp; I know cramps. I didn't sprain my knee either. Sure, I did fall many times and hit many obstacles, but I had never felt pain or trauma at the time. What could it be? Would it possibly be a consequence of my back injury in the car accident four months earlier? Perhaps a pinched nerve in my compressed L1 vertebra? Or could it be an attack of phlebitis? Whatever it is, it becomes plain that I cannot continue the march.

We have covered perhaps less than 10 miles since the river. Three more miles and we should be at Gbereh. By now I have fallen behind even more. Leaning on my stick and painfully dragging myself as slowly as a tortoise, I call ahead, shouting to Father Franco and Anthony. They stop and turn around with some apprehension. When I catch up, we discuss the new situation. The very real danger of the rebels pursuing us makes it urgent to find a solution. Obviously, after the long and exhausting hike, Anthony and Father Franco are unable to carry me. Since the next village is quite close, we decide that they go ahead to enlist the help of the villagers, who would in turn come back for me. On this note and with words of encouragement we part, Father Franco assuring me that help will come very soon. As they disappear into the foliage, I sit down on a stump. Before long I decide to try to gain some terrain. Clenching my teeth, I slowly drag myself up and on. By now my left leg is totally useless, and I am leaning with both hands on my alpenstock, which, fortunately, is quite a sturdy stick. My watch is no longer ticking, damaged perhaps by the swamp water and mud, or by shock from my many falls. By looking at the sun I estimate it should be around 9 a.m. I drag on for an eternity. Finally I hear voices ahead—the village. Thank God. This gives me added energy as I stumble along.

A few villagers rush forward to help me, and half carry me to the middle of the lively village of Gbereh. Here the missionaries of our Diocese, from the Mission post of Port Loko, had been running a grade school before the rebel attacks. Because of this, all in the village know about the Fathers, although not us personally. Now they stand all around us sympathizing, lamenting, and almost crying with us.

The town chief offers coffee. They call it coffee but in reality it is some sort of local tea. No matter, it tastes good. They also give us some cake and various fruits. They want to know what happened, where the rebels are, where we are going, and so forth. We, in turn want to know if they have any news of rebels in their area. They tell us no, there should be no rebels in their area at the moment, but they can never be sure. Oftentimes rebels come and go very fast, always leaving desolation behind. It has happened only a few days before. The people are worried that our presence in their midst could trigger reprisals from the rebels. We can appreciate that and apologize, but they are quick to assure us that they will assist us in any way they can.

Father Franco and Anthony talk to the chief about my condition. I have already proposed that I wait there for a few days until the pain subsides while the others proceed. But neither Father Franco nor the chief is happy with my suggestion. They don't know how the rebels would react, once they come to know that one of the missionaries was there. I appreciate the danger to the village as well as to me. Then the chief offers, "We will put the Father in a hammock and carry him as far as Bane-Loko." This is a bigger village down the path toward the Maboleh River. We thank the chief for the offer and plan to compensate the young men who will carry me the eight miles to Bane-Loko. I feel very grateful for this solution. Unfortunately, they have no bicycle to send ahead with a message for the UNAMSIL forces. They also need time to prepare the hammock for me and organize the team of eight strong men who would take turns, four at a time, carrying me in the hammock.

It is almost 10:30 before we can resume our march. I feel

both thankful and humbled for this solution to my problem. The young people carrying me are full of goodwill and even debonair. Father Franco leads at a good pace, the hammock follows, and behind us come Anthony and the strong men on stretcher duty. Several people of the village join us in the march. Villagers are always looking for company as they travel in the same direction for their own business. It's safer.

We reach Laia (Port Loko District). Father Franco informs me that it is about noon. Limba tribesmen live here together with Temmi. We stop briefly to rest (particularly for the men carrying me), and also to inquire if a bicycle is available to send someone ahead with a message. I try to stand on my feet, which I can do all right, but as soon as I try to take a step, that wicked pain in my left knee returns like a piercing arrow. I hop toward a mat spread for me and lie down next to the chief's chair. For a few minutes we exchange news about the rebels with the villagers as we had done in Gbereh and are reassured that no RUF has been seen around there lately.

Since the last rebel incursion, the Limba of this village have organized a group of local hunters, called Gbettys, as a civil defense force. Like the Mendes' Kamajors in the southwest, the Gbettys patrol the area looking for any trace of rebels and attempting to set up some sort of armed protection. However we are made to understand that rebels could materialize any time, and the danger is still real and great. The villagers live in constant fear.

Yes, they do have a bicycle, and the chief says he would be proud to render the service of sending a messenger. We scribble the message on a page from the two notebooks I am still carrying with me. It reads, "To the Commanding Officer of UNAMSIL, Port Loko: we are the two missionary Fathers held hostage by the RUF in Madina Tonko Limba. We have escaped and are now on the run toward your positions. We hope to be at Barmoi-Kasse sometime by tomorrow, Tuesday, Dec. 5. If possible, please meet us there and send a radio message to Bishop George Biguzzi in Freetown to alert him of the situation. Thank you. Frs. Franco and Victor."

We entrust the folded paper, wrapped in a small piece of plastic, to a boy, who takes it and promptly shoves it inside the fly of his pants, presumably in his underwear. With a big smile on his face and some compensation cash in his pocket, he jumps on his sturdy China-made bicycle and takes off amid the cheers of all bystanders.

The villagers offer us some food, but we are too anxious to get going and politely decline. By the time we leave Laia it's 1:30 p.m. Four more miles to reach Bane-Loko. The going is not rough for me, but I am thinking of Father Franco who, although a few years younger than me, at 63 is no longer a youngster and himself is recuperating from his fractured hip. He seems to be holding up quite well, thanks be to God. On the way I notice several burned-down huts, a sign of recent rebel presence.

The town we are heading to is a larger one. The missionaries from Port Loko, headed by Father Victor Bongiovanni, worked hard there for a school, a clinic and a number of bridges, connecting other nearby communities. In recognition for his work of development, he was crowned honorary town chief a few years earlier. The bicycle messenger will pass through there ahead of us, so we expect that the people at the village will be waiting for us. Lying in my hammock, I go over in my mind what this leg problem might be. I begin to rule out phlebitis, because now that I am lying down the pain has subsided. I remember reading that simply lying down and resting do not relieve phlebitis pain. My back injury from the car accident four months ago could be the source of the pain. Considering all the jogging, jumping, and falling of the past hours, the compression fracture I sustained could have disturbed the nerve roots exiting the lumbar disks in my vertebral column. All this occupies my mind while the valiant young men struggle to carry me on a footpath full of ups and downs.

We must be nearing the town because even before we catch sight of huts, we see people coming out in droves to meet us. People are singing and we enter the town as if in triumph. It is about 4:30 p.m. The chief, Sulaiman Bangura, is standing, waiting for us to approach his house. He embraces each one of us, invites us to sit down in his buffer, and personally helps me to sit down in his wicker armchair. Palm wine is brought in and served in big mugs. How cool and delicious!

As we are drinking, two middle-aged men in strange attire

approach us. They are shouldering submachine guns, and their trappings—ribbons, bandannas, and cartridge bandoliers— make them look just like the rebels. Chief Sulaiman, seeing the apprehension on our faces, quickly reassures us that these are the Gbettys of the civil defense force, at the service of the chief and the town, just like those of Laia, whom, however, we didn't see there. Here they are more numerous, and we notice them milling about among the people. The chief introduces these two who are the leaders: Abdul Kamara and Karim C. Samura. We shake hands. Commander Abdul Kamara says, "Father we are here. Don't be afraid. We will defend you." We thank them and I say, "You look more fearsome than the rebels!" Everyone laughs. After a while the chief invites us inside his house, so we excuse ourselves from the crowd and enter.

Once inside, Chief Sulaiman assures us that, for the moment, we are safe there. In fact, he invites us to spend the night in the village and proposes that we leave early in the morning. He would recruit another team of strong men to carry me in the hammock all the way beyond the Maboleh River into United Nations peacekeeping force territory. Moreover, he himself would personally accompany us with a strong group of Gbettys. In the meantime we could relax in his house, where he would have a good meal of chicken and rice prepared. We thank him warmly for his hospitality and concern. Then he excuses himself so that he can go and make arrangements for our meal. Attendants come in with large bowls of water, soap, and towels for us to wash and refresh ourselves.

Later in the evening, when we are just about ready to go to sleep, Gbettys commander Abdul Kamara bursts into the room announcing that we must leave immediately because RUF rebels might be coming during the night. As we ponder this new development, Chief Sulaiman arrives and contradicts the commander's orders, and says that it is already night and it would not be safe to travel. "Besides," he says to the commander, "the Fathers here are very tired. They are safe in this house and you will protect them in any event." Commander Kamara seems to accept the chief's decision and leaves. The chief reassures us again that everything will be all right and we should not worry. On this note he also leaves the room.

We settle down to go to sleep in the guest room of the chief's house. As it often happens, when one is excessively tired (and sore) one finds it difficult to sleep well. I am having a restless sleep and nightmarish dreams.

Very early in the morning, while it is still quite dark outside, I feel better and more relaxed. As I lie awake, I hear excited voices outside, a little beyond the house. At first I pay no attention, but then their persistence arouses my interest. I wonder what the commotion is all about. Father Franco is awakened by the noise as well. The night before we were a little disturbed by the commander's words. Now the apprehension returns. The voices are getting closer and becoming clearer. The excitement is about the choice of the route to follow in taking us to the Maboleh

River. We try to make sense out of the argument.

Apparently there are two ways for reaching our destination to the Maboleh. The more direct one, following the main footpath, would take us past the large town of Sendugu and then to the Mabanta ferry. Another way, considerably longer and less traveled, would take us through bush areas and swamps back in the direction of the Little Scarcies. After a long stretch alongside that big river, we would cut back toward the Maboleh and cross it by boat about five miles west of Mabanta.

A noisy group of Gbettys insist that we should take this second way because, they are shouting, although longer and more difficult, we would be less likely to be intercepted by the RUF, whereas on the direct way, we could be followed by rebels who might be chasing us. At one point we detect the voice of the chief who is completely opposed to taking us the longer way. It seems that the Gbettys' Commander Kamara is on his side.

As these voices right outside the chief's house grow louder and more excited, we suddenly hear the report of two rifle shots, discharged not too far from the village. Father Franco jumps up and I pull myself to my feet. At the blast of the firing, the din of the voices immediately ceases. Presently the chief comes into the room and says, "Quickly, let's go. No time to lose, follow me."

As we step outside, the discussion of the Gbettys resumes, but the chief motions us to follow him. I discover I can walk a little, although limping badly, and follow the chief, Father Franco,

Anthony, and a small group of Gbettys. After less than 200 yards a group of young men run after me with the hammock calling, "Father, Father, wait! Here, lie down here, we'll carry you." I turn around and meet them with a big smile and get on the hammock. They pick me up and at a fast pace join the group down the main footpath. During the walk the chief, flanked by Commander Kamara, begins explaining what has happened.

"My Gbettys are quite good, but we are afraid that there may be some in their midst who are in cahoots with the rebels. Last night someone came to report that the RUF could be coming and wanted you to leave right away. I thought that was strange because, with many of my men on the lookout, we had had no reports of rebels in our area. I became suspicious and prevented them from taking you the long way in the night.

"This morning some of the Gbettys were still insisting that we should take you the long way, saying that on the main footpath there might be an RUF ambush. My suspicions grew stronger. They might have wanted to go the longer way precisely because it was more likely that the rebels, informed by messengers, would be waiting by the Little Scarcies.

"My opinion was prevailing even before those two shots, which sounded to me like a signal. Why would anyone, with an AK-47, shoot twice into the air in our village at that time of the morning? That convinced me that we had to leave without delay. If there were a plot, we wouldn't give them time to execute it. I think this way is safer and keeping this pace, we will be at the

Maboleh River before noon."

We thank the chief for his care and concern and express our worry that in protecting us, he might draw the vengeance of the rebels against his town. He discounts this. "You Fathers are spending your whole life and risking it for our sake. It's only fair we do something for you." Commander Kamara adds, "Don't worry, Father, we know how to handle our people." We are impressed by the loyalty of these villagers who are taking a big risk in helping us escape.

I admire Father Franco's stamina and feel both ashamed and mortified that I, who have walked much farther than the length of this trip and have endured greater stress, should be carried in the comfort of a hammock, while my porters are straining and dripping with sweat. I suppose this situation serves to remind me of my frailty and dependence upon others.

The march is long and nonstop. The chief has arranged for 16 porters, double the previous team, so every 20 minutes four are replaced with rested ones. Thus the pace never slows.

By 10:00 we reach Sendugu, a town even bigger than Gbane Loko. Here too the missionary Fathers of Port Loko are well known and liked by the population and their Mission post was flourishing. They had a school and a clinic here before the attack of the RUF caused the Fathers to flee and the school and clinic to close. The team rests for a good hour at the house of the local chief. Food is prepared for all of us, and many people come to sympathize and wish us well. Since I feel better standing on my legs, I attempt to take a few steps and the pain in my left knee, now extended to the whole leg and foot, stabs me like a dagger. I resign myself to being carried again. Around 1 p.m. we resume our march.

After two hours of uneventful trotting, we finally reach the Maboleh River. A ferry that was operating before the war, is abandoned on the bank. The steel cables are still there, rusting and hanging from the ferry, half in the water, half on the bank. Boats now transport people and merchandise across the river. On the other side, Mabanta town, lies our freedom: an area patrolled by the United Nations peacekeeping force.

Here our party stops. We take leave of Chief Sulaiman, the Gbettys of Gbane Loko, and my porters. None of them wants compensation, but Anthony, Father Franco, and I insist that the porters at least take some small reward in money as a token of our gratefulness for their sweat and strain. Everyone is happy, and several want me to write down their names so I would remember them and tell the world how much they were suffering because of the rebels. They express the hope that after a proper period of rest in our country, we would return to Sierra Leone to continue the work we have been doing in their villages for so many years.

We embrace Chief Sulaiman. Indeed, we cannot overestimate his role in helping us to reach this point safely. A boat is ready for us. We settle in and, waving goodbye, we leave behind the land that cost us so much anxiety and pain.

CHAPTER FIFTEEN

Return to Freedom

The crossing of the river was uneventful. The three of us: Father Franco, Anthony, and I formed a group with seven other people, men and women, each carrying bundles of their merchandise along with two goats. Our group was second in line waiting for the one boat, which took about 10 minutes to cross and another 10 to return.

When we reached the other bank, I found that with the help of a stick I could walk, albeit very painfully and slowly. We climbed the steep path, some 200 yards, leading up to the plateau where the town of Mabanta lay. We had reached "free" territory from where the RUF had withdrawn months before. Although I could see no trace of the UN peacekeeping force, the people's carefree behavior was reassuring.

I sat under the shade of a large oak tree on a massive boulder overlooking the river on the north and the town on the south. Right there, on the edge of the sprawling town was a busy, typical African market — a jumble of shacks, benches, stands, and stalls crowded by a milling conglomeration of men, women, and children all crisscrossing, while chatting, calling, and laughing. Anthony purchased some bananas for us to enjoy. What a pleasant, relaxing din after the tension of only a few hours before on the other side of the river!

At one corner of the market a large Bedford seven-ton truck, parked in the middle of a dusty, dirt road not much wider than the truck itself, was taking on passengers and merchandise for a trip to Gbinti. From there some of the passengers would stay on to Batkanu, while others would get off and take other means to Lunsar and to Port Loko. The truck seemed overloaded; yet after negotiating with the apprentice boy, passengers still piled in. As the engine revved up and the truck started to move, Anthony ran up and flagged it down. The truck stopped. After a few moments of an excited exchange with Anthony, the driver shut off the engine, alighted and followed Anthony toward us.

As they approached, we heard Anthony explaining our situation, "We have just escaped from the RUF. We need to reach Barmoi-Kasseh, where we are to meet the United Nations soldiers. This town was just a few miles down the road toward Gbinty. The driver seemed to understand and sympathize. He motioned us to follow him. As we neared the truck, he shouted in Temne to the two passengers occupying the front seat, " Move to the back," while motioning to Father Franco and me to climb in. I couldn't determine for sure whether Anthony had negotiated a fare for us, but I didn't think so. While were settling down in the banged up cabin, I wondered where the two previous occupants and Anthony were going to be accommodated, since it seemed to me that the back was full as an egg, with no space even for a pin to drop. Yet, in typical African fashion, they did manage to squeeze in behind.

The heavily overloaded truck began crawling along very slowly and eventually reached a speed of 20 to 25 miles per hour, an estimate because the speedometer and other dials were either broken or missing. At first the truck spewed out a dense black smoke, which eventually turned into white, pervading the whole back almost to the cabin. After a good 45 minutes of riding past burnt down houses and farms, we reached the small town of Barmoi-Kasseh, which sat at the junction of the road to Gbinty on the east and Port Loko road on the south. At about 1:30 p.m. the driver stopped at the crossroad, right in front of a health clinic. We, and a number of others, alighted under a scorching tropical sun. The two previously displaced passengers quickly returned to their front seat, and we offered them our sincere apologies and thanks. Amid farewells for us from all (how fast the news of our situation spread among the passengers in that short ride), the truck continued toward Gbinti, after taking on a few more travelers.

We looked for the UN soldiers, but couldn't see any. We entered the veranda of the crowded clinic and were given a place to sit down, so at least we were out of the fierce sun. The appearance of us two white men caused surprise and commotion, and word of our identity and situation spread fast. Even before we could open our mouths to ask for information about the UN soldiers, people began to press around, sympathizing and offering congratulations.

We were offered water to drink. After several minutes of questions and answers about rebels' whereabouts, someone finally gave some information about the UN soldiers. They were not stationed in Barmoi-Kasseh, nor were they patrolling that area, but they would come around occasionally or if sent for. The UN considered that area not 100 percent safe and too far from their headquarters in Port Loko to be patrolled on a regular basis.

We told them that the day before we had sent ahead a messenger by bicycle. After a few moments of hesitation a young man said that two hours earlier he had seen a bicycle passing by, heading toward Hagbantama in the Port Loko direction. Perhaps that was our messenger. Someone suggested dispatching another courier by motorcycle if we could provide money for the fuel.

As I was negotiating through Anthony the cost of some fuel, I heard engines outside. With the crowd pressing around us, we couldn't see the road. Immediately we stood and made our way outside through the crowd. I was limping badly. Four soldiers in sharp military attire were alighting from a Land Rover and a Toyota Land Cruiser. Three were white men and one was black.

The black officer rushed forward excitedly shouting, "Father Victor! Father Victor!" He hugged me repeatedly and held me tight. At first I didn't recognize him, but when I was able to disengage and look him in the face, I recognized Kasibulo James Yansaneh, a Catholic young man who was a second-year college student when I left him in school four years earlier. Now he was a lieutenant of the new Sierra Leone army, seconded as liaison officer to the largely Nigerian UN peacekeeping force detachment in Port Loko. He kept on thanking God for finding me safe and sound. He introduced me as his Father to the other officers, whose names I cannot recall: one a British captain, another a Croatian lieutenant, and the third a white South African sergeant. They shook our hands and gave us a warm welcome.

The captain offered us the choice of two kinds of cold soft drinks or lemonade. I went immediately for the lemonade. How cool and delicious it was in that stifling heat! We were urged to enter their vehicles, both air-conditioned and in top shape. UN cars and vans in Sierra Leone were known to always be of the latest brands. What a contrast to all the other vehicles we had seen during our detention, including our two almost new Toyota vans, which in less than a month had become total wrecks. I was invited to climb up into the Land Cruiser with Kasibulo and the Croatian officer.

Kasibulo was so thrilled that he kept on switching from informing me about his family—particularly his brother, another officer in the Sierra Leonean army—to asking, "What happened? Where were you kept? What did they do to you? How did you escape?" The young man was so hyped that he wouldn't give me a chance to reply to any of his questions. The Croatian officer broke in to tell me that we were going to Port Loko, where we were to meet with two very important persons: their Nigerian commander Major General B. A. Ginado and our Bishop George Biguzzi.

Radio dispatched the information of our location and status to Port Loko. The dispatcher urged us to hurry because a helicopter was waiting to fly us to Freetown. Our rescuers told us how our messenger was picked up on the evening of the very day we dispatched him. A UN patrol had encountered him on the road near Hagbantama. There they read Father Franco's message and determined our whereabouts on a map. The messenger described how one of the Fathers was in bad shape, unable to walk and being transported via a hammock. The major general then radioed his general headquarters in Freetown. There they tracked down Bishop George Biguzzi, who at the time was conducting the pastoral visit in the Mission post of Lungi, the site of the International Airport of Sierra Leone across the bay from Freetown.

The bishop, upon learning of the bad conditions of one of his missionaries and not knowing the exact nature of the problem, did two things. First he phoned UNAMSIL headquarters in Freetown and succeeded in arranging for a helicopter to fly to Port Loko and wait there for our arrival. Since it was already evening and getting dark, the operation would have to be accomplished first thing the next morning. Second, he interrupted his pastoral visit and on the morning of Dec. 5 traveled by a Lungi Mission car to Port Loko, about a three-hour drive on a bad dirt road through a forested area, intending to meet us on our arrival to the military post. He would then join us in the flight to Freetown. His driver would drive back to Lungi, carrying Anthony and two other people who had joined us in the latter part of the escape, to Lungi and on to the ferry for Freetown.

The UN headquarters in Port Loko, capital city of the district of the same name, occupied the buildings of a high school. Entering the town, we were stopped at three checkpoints within a three-mile stretch. Obviously the UN soldiers were taking no chances; we were still in a war zone and rebels might infiltrate. Despite a lot of destruction and burned-down houses, a relatively busy crowd of townspeople were milling about. It was a good sign that life was returning after the hurricane of the rebel invasion and warfare. For two years Port Loko had been a stronghold of the RUF. But the combined forces of the various civil defense groups such as Kamajors, Gbettys, Capras, and the UNAMSIL finally dislodged them.

As the two vehicles approached the main entrance of the school, which had now become military barracks, we could see a number of officers and soldiers gathered right in front of the main building. Standing out among them was the white-robed bishop. As we alighted from the cars, everyone came forward and greeted us warmly. Bishop George was the first. We hugged wordlessly. I was touched by such a sympathetic response, and the bishop too was moved to see how I stumbled and limped as I left the car. He told me later that upon seeing us, emaciated and drained, he felt a big lump in his throat that choked back his words. He had gone through a great deal of diplomatic maneuvering, with five different governments (the American CIA, the Italian secret service, the Sierra Leone government, the Vatican, and the Guinean military) and the RUF itself in order to secure our release, and didn't succeed. It seemed that all had been in vain. Then, after three months of fruitless efforts, Bishop George tried sending us a note instructing us to attempt an escape if at all possible. We never got that note, and when we later came to learn about it, we were glad to know that our highest authority had been in agreement with our action.

The exuberance of the young soldiers around us, inviting us in to meet the Nigerian major general, covered up the embarrassment of our emotions. We were almost swept into the hall. There, a portly middle-aged soldier, not in formal dress decorated with medals, received us with a most cordial expression. This was Major General B.A. Ginado, the commanding officer of the UNAMSIL contingent in the Port Loko District. He welcomed us and congratulated us for being out of the clutches of the RUF. He said he had a good meal prepared for us, and all those accompanying us, before the helicopter would swiftly take the two of us and the bishop to Freetown. Evening was drawing near and we should not delay too long.

The meal was delicious: an African dish of steamed rice covered with peppery groundnut *plazas* with chicken—a most generous serving! Yet the exuberance all around us, our own excitement and sense of relief, the expectation of the final leg of the adventure all conspired to keep us from enjoying the food, in spite of the fact that we were famished. I ate a little and talked a lot, responding to congratulations from all sides. I lost sight of the four who had come to meet us at Barmoi-Kasseh and brought us to Port Loko. I missed expressing thanks and saying goodbye to Kasibulo, but as time was pressing, we moved out toward the waiting helicopter. A mere 35 minutes later we landed at the general headquarters of the UNAMSIL in Freetown. The bishop's Land Cruiser with its driver was waiting for us on the tarmac. We were swiftly driven to the bishop's residence. It was 7:30 p.m., Tuesday, Dec. 5, 2000.

EPILOGUE

Behind the Scenes of our Detention

We learned from the bishop about all his efforts to get us released. He agreed that there must have been a split in the RUF camp between Brigadier General Jussu Kamara, the recognized commander in chief (the very one who held me prisoner during my first captivity in Makeni, when he was only a brigadier general) and another faction headed by Brigadier Generals Kargbo and Dennis Mingo (Alias Superman who, after a two-day fight with Brig. Gen. Jussu Kamara, freed me from my first detention by the RUF). The split was never officially admitted. Possibly it was merely a tactic that allowed the RUF to seek peace with the government of Sierra Leone while simultaneously making a last effort to export the revolution into Guinea.

Gen. Jussu Kamara apparently wanted to negotiate peace with UNAMSIL and the government of Sierra Leone. Consequently he favored conciliatory actions and proclaimed to the world that the RUF was finished with fighting in Sierra Leone and was seeking a just peace. To my knowledge of the common rebels, Gen. Jussu represented the majority of the rank and file of the movement, who were tired of the war and could see no prospect of winning militarily. They also understood that the government, pushed by the international community, was anxious and ready to compromise.

However, a small faction of the RUF (and some of General Jussu's orderlies were in cahoots with them) wanted to pursue the fighting either in Sierra Leone or in Guinea and may have received encouragement and support from outside the RUF and of Sierra Leone. Everyone should know that the revolutions both in Liberia and Sierra Leone were started and initially supported by dynamics beyond these countries. While it is difficult for anyone outside the rebel movement to determine the extent of this outside influence, I am certain that it was operating. This I could deduce from remarks, comments and indiscretions made in my hearing by many rebels, child soldiers as well as some quite highly placed.

Be that as it may, this foreign influence in exporting the revolution could not of itself explain why so many fighters (albeit a minority) wanted to carry on with the war, if not in Sierra Leone at least in Guinea. I can think of three other practical reasons, besides the foreign link, which might have prompted continued fighting.

First, some rebels, especially the bigger fish, must have realized that the atrocities and the crimes against humanity they directly committed or were committed under their command were too great for forgiveness or amnesty. Peace negotiations could have no hope for them and therefore would not be an attractive alternative.

Second, some of them, especially the younger ones, were brought up from the ages of five, six or seven, to kill, burn, loot and be drunk with drugs and physical power. This had become their way of life, and they were irretrievably lost to civilization or even humanity.

Third, many, while not intending to continue fighting forever, hoped to profit a little more by further looting and scavenging before laying down their weapons. Then they would withdraw from the revolution, which was now foreign to them since it had moved to Guinea. They would sell their weapons to the Guineans, make some more money, and return to Sierra Leone incognito and rich.

The effort to export the revolution to Guinea did take place, but it was unsuccessful because the Guinean army was able to frustrate the rebels' initial attempts. This blocked their advance and prevented them from gaining a foothold or forming significant bases in Guinea. It is to be hoped that the revolution there will die, if it is not already dead, and that other means will be thought out and vigorously implemented in order to correct the great injustices going on in that country.

In any case, I feel that it was this last effort of the RUF to export the revolution into Guinea that caused my second capture and an additional three-month detention. This smaller faction of the RUF captured me and Father Franco in Guinea while in Sierra Leone the main RUF body, under General Jussu, was trying to make peace. The leaders of this faction, Brigadier Generals Kargbo and Mingo, frustrated the efforts of General Jussu, who under the prompting of the bishop, tried to free us. In this context it is clearer why our captors attempted to literally sell us off to the Guinean rebels.

The Immediate Aftermath of our Escape

After our arrival in Freetown, Father Franco and I spent 17 days getting organized to fly out of the country. I needed immediate medical attention. After exhaustive medical tests I was informed that my pain was caused by an acute onset of gout! When I protested to the doctor that I'd never had gout before, he remarked, "There is always a first time." Sure enough. But what an ill-fated first time—just when I was running for my life!

We both needed to buy necessities such as clothing, toiletries and traveling bags. Above all we needed to obtain identification and travel documents. All we had when we arrived in Freetown was the tattered clothing we were wearing. The travel documents took the longest time to obtain, given that because of the war neither the U.S. nor the Italian embassies in Freetown were then properly organized to issue passports.

During these 17 days people passing by gave us pieces of news about those who were in Madina during our escape. As expected, the first to discover our flight was the catechist David Yillah. He came into the church at around seven and saw the candlestick out of place on the altar. As he went to rearrange it, he saw the letter under it addressed to the RUF but not sealed. He read it and realized the seriousness of the matter. He was tempted to run, knowing that he and the Mission boys would be suspected of aiding our escape. He called the three boys who slept in the Mission and together they decided not to run, lest that be found even more incriminating and endanger their families. They decided to report our flight to Captain Kelvin. The boys were apprehended and arrested immediately.

At the same time a party was organized to chase us on the most likely escape route, the road toward Kukuna on the Guinean border only eight miles away. They set out on foot at about 8 a.m. By 11 a.m. they were back, satisfied that we hadn't gone that way. Another party then followed the very direction we had taken, but they did not return, not until very late at night. Not only could they not trace us, but they had gotten lost and returned frustrated, angry, and fearful that the High Command in Makeni would hold them responsible for not being able to catch up with us. The leaders in Madina who knew about my back injury felt certain that we could not have gone very far and were perhaps hiding in the surrounding villages.

The rebels' frustration was vented on five of the young men considered the closest to us—the three Mission boys, the catechist, and another friend of theirs. They stripped them naked and beat them mercilessly, demanding to know where we were hiding.

In the meantime the RUF High Command in Makeni, alerted by radio, summoned Cols. Joe and Matthew and interrogated them about our escape, suspecting that they had had a hand in it, since they both were Catholic and had always shown great respect and even sympathy toward us. Subsequently they were cleared of any responsibility.

Three of the RUF guards who should have been on duty that night were charged with treason, along with Capt. Kelvin and David the catechist. They were court-martialed and ordered to be shot. When we heard this, Father Franco decided to write a letter to General Jussu, reiterating what he had written in the statement left under the candle, which said that no one in Madina had any knowledge or hand in our escape. If the execution of those four was carried out, we would approach the international media and reveal to the world all that had been going on behind RUF lines, including their involvement in Guinea and their repeated attacks there which we witnessed in Pamelap and in Madina. This was probably the strongest argument that could be used to save those people. We had always told the rebels that if they released us, we wouldn't use against them anything we had witnessed during our detention. We kept our promise, even though we weren't bound by it since they did not release us. Because we didn't wish to jeopardize the innocent who were involved with the rebels, we refused to make any statement to the media. Ten days after our escape the rebels must have realized that we had not made any accusations.

The bishop forwarded this letter to the general with whom he had direct contacts because of his intermediary function. As it was hoped and expected, the letter obtained the intended effect. The court martial was changed to public flogging to blood. The fact that at that time the RUF was engaged in convincing the world of their good faith and that they weren't interested in exporting the revolution into Guinea, made our threats very powerful and effective. We were gratified to know that we had saved the lives of those people.

Eventually we were able to get travel documents from the American embassy for me, and from the Italian embassy for Father Franco. With those, we were able to take off for Europe on Dec. 23, 2000, on a Sabena Airways flight. However, I didn't reach my destination until the evening of the day after Christmas. I had to spend all of Christmas Eve stranded in the Brussels airport because a heavy snowstorm shut down all airports in northern Europe and resulted in the cancellation of all flights. I huddled on a bench in the Brussels airport, nearly freezing in my tropical clothes, hoping that, after having escaped death by the RUF of Sierra Leone, I would not die of cold in Europe! My time had not yet come. Thank goodness — because I had plans for a return to my Mission to continue witnessing the Gospel of Jesus among those tormented people of God.

Update of Events

The civil war ended in 2002 with the rebels laying down their arms and the government granting amnesty to the combatants. Then the Demobilization, Disarmament, and Reintegration program (DDR) was organized under the auspices of the UNAMSIL troops, who would guarantee its proper and smooth implementation. The Peace and Reconciliation

Commission (TRC) was instituted on the model of the South African initiative, where citizens were encouraged to come forward and voluntarily confess any wrongdoing inflicted or suffered during the war period and be reconciled with one another.

The UN, in collaboration with the government of Sierra Leone, created a special tribunal for war crimes and crimes against humanity, perpetrated by the main leaders of the combatants on all sides of the conflict — RUF, CDF, and deserters from the Sierra Leone Army (SLA), nicknamed the "West Side Boys."

Corporal Foday Sanko, the founder and supreme leader of the RUF, was the first arrested and referred to this tribunal and while being tried, died in prison of natural causes. Some of the more famous (or infamous?) leaders of the RUF have been killed or died at large, among them Field Commander-in-Chief Sam Bukari (alias Mosquito), Brigadier General Dennis Mingo (alias Superman), Colonel Kumba (alias Papazumba). Also reported dead was Johnny Paul Koroma, ex-captain in the Sierra Leone Army, who overthrew the legitimate government of Alhaji Tijan Kabba and installed himself as chairman of the AFRC (Armed Forces Revolutionary Council) and Head of State, calling the RUF rebels to participate in his government.

Others main leaders of the RUF and the CDF were arrested and are currently in prison. Their trial by the UN Special Court for Sierra Leone began on July 5, 2004. Among the defendants there are some who have been directly connected with our capture and detention. The last to join this list in April 2006 was former rebel leader and ex-president of Liberia, Charles Taylor. He was arrested for his role in instigating and aiding the RUF in Sierra Leone, thus becoming accomplice to their human atrocities and war crimes.

The awful toll of the 11-year conflict includes about 75,000 civilians killed, 20,000 mutilated, 5,400 children abducted and coerced into fighting, or otherwise forced into labor and sex exploitation, countless victims of rape and other abuses. About 80 percent of Sierra Leone's 5 million citizens became displaced or refugees and most of the already meager infrastructure of the country was destroyed (hospitals, clinics, schools, roads and bridges, government office structures, communication facilities like TV and radio stations, telephone equipment, and so on).

Presently the reconstruction of the country has begun in earnest. International NGOs have returned in strength. Catholic missionaries resumed their apostolic and charitable work. Father Franco Manganello, SX, has returned to Sierra Leone to the very Mission post at Madina, where he was detained with me under house arrest, thus fulfilling the promise he made in the letter to the rebels the night of our escape: "We are not running away from you, we are going only to return and render you the service we cannot do now because of our confinement."

As this book goes to print, I am still in the U.S. in spite of repeated requests to my superiors to allow me to return to my beloved Sierra Leone. Currently I minister at Catholic Student Centers (Newman Centers) in colleges and universities in the Midwest. My religious community, the St. Francis Xavier Foreign Missions Society (The Xaverian Missionaries) asked me to promote Catholic foreign missions awareness among students especially by telling my story. We hope and pray that God inspires some young people who learn of my love for God and mission work to pursue the same path in my missionary congregation, or any other. It is only with this hope and with the support and encouragement of my community in Franklin, Wis., that this 30-year veteran missionary is willing to sacrifice his yearning to return where he left his heart.

The End

About the Xaverian Missionaries

The international religious congregation called the St. Francis Xavier Foreign Mission Society (The Xaverian Missionaries) is in the United States specifically to promote the missionary idea of St. Francis Xavier as understood by the founder of the society, Blessed Guido Maria Conforti, bishop of Parma, Italy. This ideal is made up of two distinct, if very related, aspects:

1. Make all baptized Christians aware that as followers of Christ, they are mandated to spread the Kingdom of God on earth. This is done by acting as a Christian witness in the world they live in. This in turn, through the Communion of the saints, will draw God's grace to those without Faith in mission lands.

2. Inspire through their apostolic work, community life, and preaching particularly among young people the vocation to follow God's call to actively spread His Kingdom on earth in foreign lands, or foreign mission territories, as missionary priests, brothers and or even lay volunteers.

As this book goes to press, about 900 missionary priests, brothers and professed students of the Xaverian Missionary Society serve in 20 countries and four continents. Their world motherhouse remains in Parma, Italy. National centers are located throughout the world.

In traditionally Christian countries where the Xaverians are present (Italy, Spain, France, Great Britain, the United States, Mexico, Brazil, Columbia and the Philippines), their activity hinges mostly on promoting missionary awareness and organizing seminaries (at college and theology level) and novitiates to prepare young men for consecrated life in the mission field.

In non-Christian countries (Burundi, Cameroon, Chad, Mozambique, Democratic Republic of Congo, Sierra Leone, Bangladesh, Indonesia, Japan, and Taiwan), the Xaverians are dedicated to announcing and spreading the message of Jesus' love and salvation with respect to the needs of the local populations, within their cultures, religions, and customs. In this context the Xaverians establish and run churches, schools, hospitals, clinics and social programs to promote human development and welfare, justice and peace.

For More Information
Web site: www.xaviermissionaries.org

Vocation Director:
Fr. Adolph Menendez, SX
adolphmenendez@yahoo.com
(414) 243.22.48

GLOSSARY and ABBREVIATIONS

AFRC - Armed Forces Revolutionary Council

CDF - Civil Defense Forces (Mende: Kamajors; Temni: Kapras; Kuranko: Tamaboros; Kono: Donsos; Limba: Gbettys)

DDR - Disarmament, Demobilization, Reintegration Program

ECOMOG - Economic Community of West African States Monitoring Group

ECOWAS - Economic Community of West African States

Krio - Lingua franca of most people in Sierra Leone. It is the proper language of the Creoles, the descendents of the freed slaves from the UK, who settled in the Western area peninsula

Kuranko - One of the 14 ethnic groups and local language in Sierra Leone

Limba - One of the 14 ethnic groups and local language in Sierra Leone

Mende - The largest of the 14 ethnic groups (tribes) and language in Sierra Leone

MSF - Medicins Sans Frontiers (Doctors Without Borders)

NPRC - National Provisional Ruling Council

RFDG - Rassemblement des Forces Democratique de Guinee (the rebels of Guinea)

RSLMF - Republic of Sierra Leone Military Forces

RUF - Revolutionary United Front, rebels of Sierra Leone

SLA - Sierra Leone Army (The original Sierra Leone Army, disbanded by President Tijan Kabba during the civil war because it was infested by deserters and traitors)

TRC - Truth and Reconciliation Committee

Temni - The second largest ethnic group (tribe) and language in Sierra Leone

UNAMSIL - United Nations Armed Mission in Sierra Leone